A PILGRIM'S JOURNEY

A PILGRIM'S JOURNEY

The Autobiography
of
Ignatius of Loyola

Introduction, Translation, and Commentary
by
Joseph N. Tylenda, S.J.

Revised Edition

IGNATIUS PRESS   SAN FRANCISCO

Cover art by Christopher J. Pelicano
Cover design by Roxanne Mei Lum

CONTENTS

Appendices

INTRODUCTION

I. "The Pilgrim's Journey"

Sometime during the year 1552, two of Ignatius of Loyola's closest associates, Juan de Polanco and Jerónimo Nadal, made a special request of him.[1] Now that Ignatius had finished writing the Constitutions of the Society of Jesus, and since Ignatius' health had been growing progressively worse, both friends feared that they would not long have their beloved Founder with them. Thus they asked him to leave his followers "some admonition as a testament" that would show them the way to virtue. Other founders of religious orders had done this,[2] and Polanco and Nadal thought it behooved Ignatius to do the same. With this in mind, Nadal approached Ignatius and requested him to narrate how God had guided him from the first days of his conversion until the present. To Nadal's way of thinking, such a description of the divine action in Ignatius' soul would at the same time describe the founding of the Society of Jesus.

Ignatius was reluctant to yield to their request—he was always unwilling to talk about himself. Though his colleagues continued to urge him to compose this testament, Ignatius procrastinated. He changed his mind only after Luis Gonçalves da Câmara met him in the garden adjacent to their Roman residence, on August 4, 1553, and spoke with him.

---

[1] See Preface, no. 1, and Appendix I, no. 2.

[2] See, for example, "The Testament of St. Francis", in *St. Francis of Assisi: Writings and Early Biographies*, ed. Marion A. Habig (Chicago: Franciscan Herald, 1973), 67–70.

Gonçalves da Câmara was a Portuguese, born about 1519, and the son of the governor of Madeira. In 1535 he went to Paris to study languages and philosophy, and there he met Pierre Favre and the other companions and manifested an interest in their enterprise. Ignatius had already left Paris for his return visit to Spain. After concluding his studies, Gonçalves da Câmara returned to Portugal and entered the Society in Lisbon on April 27, 1545. In 1553 he was summoned to Rome to report on the state of the Society in Portugal and arrived in the Eternal City on May 23. In Rome he was appointed minister of the Jesuit residence and remained there until October 23, 1555, when he left Rome for Portugal.[3]

In their chat in the garden, Gonçalves da Câmara spoke to Ignatius about vainglory. While telling him the means to overcome it, Ignatius thought back to his own pre-conversion days, when vanity had dictated his every action. Perhaps the sixty-two-year-old Ignatius saw himself in the thirty-four-year-old Luis struggling against vanity, and while Polanco and Nadal had been unsuccessful in their attempt to get him to reveal his interior life to them, this Portuguese Jesuit unknowingly succeeded. Ignatius realized that if he were to narrate the journey he had made from a vain courtier to a humble pilgrim seeking only God, it might not only help Gonçalves da Câmara to overcome his present inclination to vainglory, but it might also help others. Thus, Ignatius chose him as the one to whom he would describe his pilgrim journey.

---

[3] Gonçalves da Câmara again returned to Rome in May 1558 to attend the first General Congregation called to elect Ignatius' successor. During the congregation he was elected assistant for Portugal to Diego Laínez, the new Father General. On July 3, 1559, he left Rome for Portugal to be tutor to the youthful King Sebastian and died in Lisbon on March 15, 1575.

Ignatius began the narration of his life's story toward the end of August 1553, just a couple of weeks after he had made the decision to do so. Though Gonçalves da Câmara states in his Preface that Ignatius dictated this material, he does not mean to say that he served as an amanuensis, there and then recording each and every word Ignatius uttered. During Ignatius' narration he listened attentively, but only after he had left Ignatius and had gone to his room did he jot down, in brief or outline form, what he had heard. Some time later—was it days or weeks?—he enfleshed these notes and read them to a Spanish scribe, who then recorded them verbatim. Gonçalves da Câmara insists in his Preface that he tried "not to write a single word other than those that I have heard from the Father",[4] and Nadal assures us in his Preface that Gonçalves da Câmara was "endowed with an excellent memory".[5] Even with such an excellent memory there are a few inconsistencies between what Gonçalves da Câmara wrote in his Preface and what is found in the text itself.[6]

Ignatius interrupted his narrative sometime in September 1553, having reached, at that time, his first days in Manresa. This interruption lasted seventeen months, and it was only on March 9, 1555, that he returned to telling his story, but then, due to the death of Pope Julius III on March 23, the narration was again put off. This second interruption lasted

---

[4] See his Preface, no. 3.

[5] See Appendix I, no. 4.

[6] For example, in his Preface, no. 2, he seems to say that Ignatius began his narration in September 1553, while in no. 10 of the text he says that it was already in progress in August 1553. Also, his Preface, no. 5, says that his last meeting with Ignatius was on the eve of his departure. Since he left Rome on October 23, 1555, that would mean that the final meeting had taken place on October 22, but in no. 99 of the text he seems to indicate that the last meeting with Ignatius was on October 20.

six months. Since Ignatius decided on September 21, 1555, that Gonçalves da Câmara was to return to Portugal, there was now some urgency for him to conclude what he had begun. Gonçalves da Câmara met with him on September 22 and continued until October 20 (according to the text) or October 22 (according to the Preface). The material collected during this third period of narration remained in the form of abbreviated notes until Gonçalves da Câmara arrived in Genoa in November 1555. While awaiting passage to Spain, he took the notes he had made the month before, prepared them, and dictated the remainder of the text to an Italian scribe, since no Spanish scribe was available. Thus, the first two-thirds of the text was written in Spanish and the final third in Italian.

The text covers but eighteen of Ignatius' sixty-five years. It begins with his wounding at the siege of Pamplona (1521) and describes his conversion at Loyola, his growth in the spiritual life through the extraordinary graces he received at Manresa, his pilgrimage to the Holy Land, his decision to study, and his life in Barcelona, Alcalá, Salamanca, and Paris. Finally, unable to go to the Holy Land, Ignatius and companions traveled to Rome to place themselves at the disposal of the pope (1538). Ignatius' first thirty years—that is, his youth and life as a courtier—are not included in the text, but a resumé of that portion of his life is given in the second part of this Introduction. Likewise, the remaining seventeen years of his life in Rome as Father General of a new religious order are outside the text and are treated in the third part of this Introduction.

The text that Gonçalves da Câmara dictated to the two Spanish scribes in Rome, and to the Italian scribe in Genoa, is no longer extant. Several copies of that Spanish-Italian text, however, were made at a very early date, for Nadal had such a copy and carried it with him on his visits to the various Jesuit houses. Sometime between 1558 and 1561, Father Annibal du Coudret, a Frenchman then stationed in Rome, translated the Spanish-Italian text into Latin, and since Nadal appears to have been unaware that Gonçalves da Câmara had already written a preface to the text, he wrote his own (see Appendix I). And since the text was without a title, Nadal gave it one, calling it *The Acts of Father Ignatius, as Father Luis Gonçalves First Wrote Them, Receiving Them from the Mouth of the Father Himself.*

Du Coudret's Latin translation of the text was the first to be published, namely, in the *Acta Sanctorum* (vol. 34: *Julii,* tom. 7 [1731]). The Spanish-Italian text was first published in 1904, in the *Monumenta Ignatiana: Scripta de Sancto Ignatio de Loyola,* 1 (Madrid). This was the first critical edition. Another critical edition, together with du Coudret's Latin translation, appeared in *Fontes Narrativi de S. Ignatio de Loyola,* 1: *Narrationes scriptae ante annum 1557* (Rome: Monumenta Historica Soc. Iesu, 1943). This edition, together with that of Candido de Dalmases, S.J., in *Obras completas de San Ignacio de Loyola* (Madrid: Biblioteca de Autores Cristianos, 1982), provide the basis for our present English translation.

To date[7] five English translations have appeared. In 1900 two were published almost simultaneously; that of E. M. Rix, *The Testament of Ignatius Loyola* (London), and that of J. F. O'Conor, S.J., *The Autobiography of St. Ignatius* (New York, Benziger). Both of these translations were made prior to the publication of the critical Spanish-Italian text and relied exclusively on du Coudret's Latin version in the *Acta Sanctorum.* All subsequent translations have been based on the critical text. In 1956 William J. Young, S.J., offered his

---

[7] That is, prior to the first appearance of the present translation in 1985.

translation, calling it *St. Ignatius' Own Story: As Told to Luis González de Cámara* (Chicago, Regnery), and in 1974 there followed *The Autobiography of St. Ignatius Loyola* (New York, Harper and Row), translated by Joseph F. O'Callaghan. Then came that of Parmananda R. Divarkar, *A Pilgrim's Testament: The Memoirs of Ignatius of Loyola* (Rome: Gregorian University, 1983).[8]

With these several translations, why another one? Inasmuch as the story that Ignatius tells is brief, compact, and somewhat incomplete, the text really calls for a commentary, which Ignatius' contemporaries would certainly have been able to supply but not so the modern reader. Furthermore, a commentary is needed to explain the various allusions in the text, to clarify some of its ambiguities, and, in general, to give the reader a fuller-flowing biographical sketch of the Founder of the Jesuits and thus serve as a complement to the text. Since such a commentary had up to now not been written, it was therefore deemed necessary, and a new translation was also prepared at the same time, for only by wrestling with the Spanish-Italian text does one come close to Ignatius and become better equipped to write a commentary. The commentary that follows is heavily dependent upon the abundant historical data supplied by Candido de Dalmases, S. J., in both his 1943 and 1982 critical editions.

---

[8] Two translations have appeared subsequent to the first publication of the present translation. Antonio T. de Nicolas' "Autobiography: Also Known as Diary of a Pilgrim (1521–1538)", which forms part of his *Powers of Imagining: Ignatius de Loyola. A Philosophical Hermeneutic of Imagining through the Collected Works of Ignatius de Loyola with a Translation of These Works* (Albany: State University of New York, 1986), 239–97, 370–73, and the translation by Philip Endean, which he entitles "Reminiscences or Autobiography of Ignatius Loyola" in his and J. A. Munitiz' *Saint Ignatius of Loyola: Personal Writings* (London: Penguin, 1996), 12–64, 361–77.

Since Gonçalves da Câmara never gave a title to the text he produced, it remained for later editors and translators to add their own. As previously noted, Nadal called it the *Acts* of Ignatius, since it delineated Ignatius' life and deeds over a period of eighteen years. Both O'Conor and O'Callaghan have called it Ignatius' *Autobiography*, and such it is, since Ignatius narrates his life history. Young paraphrases that idea and calls it Ignatius' *Testament*, since this was what Nadal and Polanco had requested of him, and Divarkar calls it *A Pilgrim's Testament*, joining the fact that this was Ignatius' testament to his sons and the fact that in the text Ignatius refers to himself in the third person and frequently calls himself "the pilgrim".

I have entitled this translation *The Pilgrim's Journey*, taking into account that "pilgrim" is what Ignatius called himself and that throughout his life he was on a pilgrimage seeking God. The journey he made during those years was not merely a land and sea journey to the Holy Land and through Europe; more importantly, it was a spiritual journey that he had embarked upon. After his conversion, Ignatius sought God and God alone. He left Loyola in order to seek God in the Holy Land, and he ends his narration saying: "At whatever time or hour he wanted to find God, he found Him" (no. 99).

In the present edition the translation of Gonçalves da Câmara's text appears in the upper portion of the page with the commentary in the lower portion. The numbering of the paragraphs coincides in text and commentary.

II. Early Life of Ignatius of Loyola, 1491–1520

Ignatius, the seventh and youngest son of Beltrán Ibáñez de Oñaz y Loyola and Marina Sánchez de Licona, was born in the family castle in Azpeitia, in the Basque province of Guipúzcoa in northern Spain. He was baptized in the parish church of San Sebastián de Soreasu and was given the name Iñigo López. Iñigo was a common name among the Basques, and it recalled the saintly Benedictine Abbot of Oña, who died in 1057. The López part of his name derived from one of his ancestors. For the first forty-five years or so of his life he was known as Iñigo, and only while in Paris was his name, and not by his own doing, changed to Ignatius. It appears that the university officials, unaware that the Latin form of Iñigo was *Enecus*, latinized his Basque name into *Ignatius*. The earliest use of this version of the name occurs in the 1531 rector's book listing the students matriculated at the university.[9] This is also the way his name appears on his master's diploma. Eventually, with the entrance of many non-Spaniards into the Society, Iñigo adopted *Ignatius* as his name.

The recognized year of Ignatius' birth is 1491, but since his baptismal record had been destroyed by fire, the exact date of his birth is lost to history. In narrating the events of his life to Gonçalves da Câmara, Ignatius says (no. 1) that he was twenty-six at the time of the siege of Pamplona (1521), which would mean that he was born in 1495. The text later states (no. 30) that he was sixty-two years old in 1555, which would then have him born in 1493. When the early Jesuits attempted to solve this discrepancy and approached the woman who had nursed him in infancy, they asked her whether Ignatius was actually sixty-two in 1555. The woman immediately corrected them,

---

[9] In the *Acta Rectoria Universitatis Parisiensis* for 1531 we find "Ignacio de loyola, pampinol.", and in that for 1534 we read "Dominus Ignatius de Loyola, dioc. pampilonensis". See Gabriel María Verd, "De Iñigo a Ignacio: El cambio de nombre en San Ignacio de Loyola", *Archivum Historicum Societatis Iesu* 60 (1991), 113–60, especially 130.

saying that Ignatius was two years older, meaning that he had been born in 1491.[10] Since the woman was already advanced in years, there was the possibility that her memory might have been faulty. But many years later a legal document, drawn up by a notary in Azpeitia, was happily discovered. The document is dated October 23, 1505, and mentions that Iñigo of Loyola acted as a witness in the sale of a horse.[11] Since the law of Castile and Guipúzcoa stipulates that no male who had not passed his fourteenth birthday could validly act as a witness in a legal matter, it follows that our Iñigo of Loyola was born sometime prior to October 23, 1491.

In addition to his six brothers, Ignatius had three sisters, and there were perhaps three other offspring of his father, but Ignatius was the youngest of all.[12] Since he had been given to María de Garín, the young wife of a blacksmith living but a short distance from the castle, to be nursed, it is generally presumed that Ignatius' mother had died when he was still an infant.[13] It is not known how long he lived with his nurse, nor is it known when he returned to live with his family in the castle. Since Juan Pérez, Ignatius' oldest brother, had died in 1496 during the Spanish campaign in Naples, Martín García, the second son, became heir to the family estate. Martín García married Magdalena de Araoz on September 11, 1498,[14] and since he brought his wife home to be the new mistress of Loyola, this

---

[10] See *IdL* 18; *PY* 26.

[11] See *FD*, doc. 32.

[12] For the names and biographies of the members of Ignatius' immediate family, see *FD* 773–94.

[13] See *PY* 25. The cottage, Eguíbar, where Ignatius lived with his nurse, still stands.

[14] *FD* 782; *GV* 51. However, *FN* 1:153 n. 5 says that the marriage took place on September 14, 1493. This date seems unlikely since Martín García was born ca. 1478, and if he married in 1493, it would mean that he had married at age fifteen.

may have been as good a time as any for Ignatius to return to
his ancestral residence. Ignatius' education at Loyola was min-
imal according to today's standard, but according to those of
that age it was deemed quite satisfactory, for he knew how to
read and write.

Among Ignatius' father's friends was Juan Velázquez de
Cuéllar, King Ferdinand's chief treasurer, whose wife, María
de Velasco, was related to Ignatius' mother. Velázquez wrote
to Ignatius' father, perhaps sometime in 1506, suggesting that
the elder Loyola might want to send one of his younger sons
to live with him at Arévalo and be educated as a Castilian
gentleman. Velázquez' invitation was readily accepted, and
the father chose to send the fifteen-year-old Ignatius to
Arévalo, some 280 miles away. Together with Velázquez' sons,
Ignatius was trained in courtly manners and learned riding
and fencing, dancing and singing, and all that was expected
of a courtier. It was also at Arévalo that he was introduced to
the literature of the day—the adventure-filled novels of chivalry. As the king's treasurer, Velázquez was frequently at court
and often traveled with it when it went to Madrid or Segovia, Valladolid, Medina del Campo, or Seville. As Ignatius
grew older and became more accustomed to courtly life, he
too was included in Velázquez' retinue.

From Ignatius' eleven or so years with Velázquez, only
one incident has come down to us. Ignatius made periodic
visits to Loyola—his father had already died in 1507—but
his visit in February 1515 became the occasion of a legal
action against him. The Loyola family was the patron of the
church of San Sebastián de Soreasu in Azpeitia, whose rector was Juan de Anchieta. Until 1515 Anchieta had been
Master of the Chapel Royal, and during that time he lived at
court, leaving the parish in the care of his vicars. But Anchieta now returned to Azpeitia and thought about retiring.

As the church's patron, the Loyola family had the right to appoint Anchieta's successor, and the family intended to grant the benefice to their priest-brother, Pero López. Disregarding the Loyolas' right to make the new appointment, Anchieta went ahead and named his nephew, García López de Anchieta, to succeed him. On Shrove Tuesday, February 20, 1515, Ignatius, Pero López, and several others, taking advantage of the fact that it was carnival time, became involved in some sort of harassment or violence directed against the parish clergy in Azpeitia. Whatever happened that evening was considered to be sufficiently serious for a legal action to be introduced against Ignatius and his brother. Some of the documents of that process are extant,[15] but none of them mentions the actual charge brought against Ignatius. Nevertheless, in the eyes of the magistrate it was considered to have been "very serious", since it had been perpetrated "during the night, with malice aforethought, and treacherously carried out by means of an ambush".[16]

In response to this legal action, both brothers, Pero López and Ignatius, appealed to clerical immunity. This was possible since Pero López was a priest and Ignatius had received the tonsure. The brothers thus claimed that they had the right to be tried by an ecclesiastical and not a secular court. It is not known when Ignatius had received the tonsure, for there is no record of it in the Pamplona diocesan archives, but it certainly must have been sometime prior to his going to Arévalo. To enjoy clerical immunity, Ignatius would have had to have worn the tonsure and clerical dress for four months immediately preceding the crime. But it was common knowledge in Azpeitia that Ignatius' tonsure was much

---

[15] See *FD*, doc. 48; *GV* 97–99.
[16] *FD* 238.

smaller than the prescribed size and that he always dressed in slashed suits of bright colors with flowing cape and wore tight-fitting colored hose and boots. A sword and dagger were at his waist, his long curly hair rested on his shoulders, and his cap proudly sported a feather. Furthermore, he was frequently seen wearing a breastplate and coat of mail. It was the magistrate's opinion that since Ignatius decked himself out in the finery of a secular soldier and not in the somber colors of the heavenly militia, he ought to stand trial before the secular court.[17]

The case against the brothers seems to have been dropped eventually, for there is no extant document explaining how it ended. But the knowledge of the scandal he once caused in Azpeitia remained with Ignatius, and in 1535, when he returned to his native land to recuperate, he chose to live there, beg his daily bread, and, thus, make reparation for his earlier unbecoming behavior.

King Ferdinand died on January 23, 1516, but prior to his death he had appointed his sixteen-year-old grandson, Charles, to act as regent for his unfortunate mother, Queen Juana la Loca. Charles was to succeed to the throne upon his mother's death, but rather than wait for nature to have its course, Charles had himself declared king on March 14, 1516, in Flanders, and then changed the provisions in his grandfather's will. While Ferdinand left a pension for his second wife, Germaine de Foix, from monies coming from Naples, Charles ordered that the monies were to come from certain Castilian towns, including Arévalo and others directly under Velázquez' authority. The citizens of these cities, and Velázquez with them, expressed their surprise and displeasure, especially since these cities had been

---

[17] For a more complete description of the legal proceedings against Ignatius, see *PY* 44–46 or *IL* 21–23.

granted the privilege of nonalienation from the Castilian crown. According to Charles' decision, these towns would now belong to Queen Germaine, who in fact was a foreigner and the niece of Louis XII, King of France. The result was that Velázquez was removed from office. He then moved to Madrid, and there he died a broken man on August 12, 1517.[18]

With Velázquez' death, Ignatius had to seek new employment. Growing sated with the life of a courtier, he now thought of following that of a soldier, seeking renown by gallantry in battle. Ignatius thus entered the service of Don Antonio Manrique de Lara, Duke of Nájera and Viceroy of Navarre.[19] In September 1520, when the townspeople of Nájera were engaged in a minor revolt against their duke, Ignatius played a major part in bringing the city back to the duke's obedience. And when there was a minor disturbance in Guipúzcoa, between the cities of San Sebastián and Hernani, the duke sent Ignatius there to bring peace to that region, which he succeeded in doing. It was while Ignatius was in Guipúzcoa that the duke urgently sent for him to return, since the French were advancing on Pamplona. Ignatius and his men rushed toward the Navarrese capital, and the events that followed his arrival form the beginning of the story that Ignatius narrated to Gonçalves da Câmara.

III. Later Life of Ignatius of Loyola, 1539–1556

Ignatius' narration to Gonçalves da Câmara ends with the year 1538. Ignatius had then been in Rome for an entire

---

[18] See *GV* 101–7.

[19] It was Velázquez' widow, María de Velasco, who suggested that Ignatius seek service with her relative Don Antonio Manrique, and on Ignatius' departure she gave him five hundred *escudos* and two horses (*GV* 114–16).

year, and since he and his companions were unable to go to the Holy Land and there labor for souls, they offered their services to Pope Paul III in November 1538. They had banded together with the express purpose of converting the infidel, but now that that goal was impossible to attain, the group was faced with a vexing problem. Should they disband, or should they remain together? If they were to remain as a group, should they remain as they were, that is, a group bound by mutual charity and dedicated to the salvation of souls, or should they form themselves into a religious congregation; and, in addition to their vows of poverty and chastity, should they take a vow to obey the individual who would be elected as their head?

With this in mind, these first Jesuits gathered in Rome in mid-March 1539 and began a series of discussions.[20] Until now they had never given any thought to the possibility of forming a new congregation in the Church. Their deliberations lasted through Lent and a good part of the Easter season. By April 15 they had unanimously decided to remain together and to form a new congregation with the vow of obedience. Discussion continued until June 24, touching on questions as to the nature of their organization, its purpose and function, whether they should undertake the running of colleges and churches, how new members should be added, and so on. Ignatius was deputed to summarize these discussions in a document that would eventually be presented to the pope. By the end of June or early July, Ignatius had completed his task, and that summary has come to be known as the "Formula of the Institute".[21] Ignatius then requested Cardinal Gasparo Contarini to submit it to the pope for his ap-

---

[20] See *GV* 462–63.

[21] For an English translation, see *FX* 462–65.

proval. The cardinal read the document to Pope Paul III on September 3, and His Holiness immediately approved it.[22] The pope then directed that the official bull approving the Society of Jesus be prepared and promulgated.

The papal bull *Regimini militantis Ecclesiae*, granting official approval to the Society, was not published until a year had passed, that is, on September 27, 1540. While the Jesuits were waiting for this approbation, they continued their usual preaching and teaching, hearing confessions and catechizing. Favre and Diego Laínez had gone to northern Italy to rekindle the faith among the Parmesans, and Simão Rodrigues and Francis Xavier had left for Portugal. Since the Society of Jesus had been officially and canonically recognized by the Holy See, it now had to draw up constitutions in accord with the apostolate described in the "Formula" and approved in the papal bull. The companions, who were then in Rome, met on March 4, 1541, and agreed that the task of writing the Constitutions should be given to Ignatius and that Jean Codure was to assist him. There was also the question of choosing one of their number as general, and so Ignatius asked all who could conveniently come to Rome to be there for the middle of Lent. Those who were unable to come because of distance were to send their vote in writing. Of the original companions, four were unable to attend: Favre was in Germany, Rodrigues and Xavier were in Portugal, and Nicolás Bobadilla in Calabria. The remaining six decided that before voting they should spend three days in prayer

---

[22] *GV* 464–65 has Cardinal Contarini's letter to Ignatius in which he tells of the pope's oral approval. Rodrigues states that the pope, after hearing the "Formula" read to him, extended his hand in blessing over the document and said: "We bless, we praise, we approve." Nadal adds that the pope also remarked: "The Spirit of God is here."

and only at the end of that period should they write down their choice for general. After these three days their votes were placed in a box together with those that had been received from those companions unable to come. They waited another three days, and then on April 8, 1541, the ballots were read. Each was a vote for Ignatius; his own ballot showed that he had voted for "the one who receives the most votes".[23]

Ignatius declined the election, insisting that since he could not govern himself, he was unable to govern others; that the sins of his past life weighed so heavily upon him that he could not take on so important a role; and, finally, that he preferred to obey rather than to command.[24] But his entreaty met deaf ears. He then asked his companions to consider the matter prayerfully for another three days. The second ballot was cast on April 13, and it confirmed the previous one. Ignatius, however, was still reluctant to accept, and so he asked for several days in which to pray and seek advice from his Franciscan confessor. Ignatius then went to the Franciscan monastery of San Pietro in Montorio, on Rome's Janiculum, and spent some days in intense prayer and consultation with his confessor.[25] The advice he received was that he had to accept the office of general of the Society, since this was the manifest will of God. Ignatius accepted the election on April 19, and on the twenty-second—it was Friday of Easter Week—he and his five companions set out to visit the seven ancient churches of Rome. When they arrived at Saint Paul Outside-the-Walls, they made their confessions to each other, and as Ignatius celebrated Mass in the Chapel of Our Lady, these six Jesuits,

---

[23] See *GV* 479.

[24] See *GV* 482.

[25] His confessor was Fr. Theodosius (*GV* 482–83).

at the moment of Communion, pronounced their vows in the newly formed Society of Jesus.[26]

At the time of his election as general, Ignatius was fifty years old. His contemporaries have described him as being somewhat small in stature but sturdily built and as walking with a limp because of the wound received at Pamplona. His face was round, with a pointed chin; his nose was aquiline, and he had a high smooth forehead with a hairline that receded with age. His eyes were said to have been deep set and cheerful; his hair was brown, with a touch of gray in it, and he kept his beard short and trimmed after the manner of the masters at the University of Paris.[27]

Ignatius had fifteen years in which to form and guide the new Society. Besides overseeing its growth and development, he spent a good part of these years writing and perfecting the Society's Constitutions. He also carried on an extensive correspondence, not only concerning what was necessary for the everyday business of the Society, but also as guidance to many individuals in the ways of the spiritual life. The Society did not limit its activity to Rome. Ignatius sent his Jesuits wherever bishops had need of them. Whether it was to northern or southern Italy, France or Germany, Spain or Portugal, the Jesuits went to instruct the people in the faith and to give the Spiritual Exercises to all whom they judged ready. These Jesuits carried God's word from city to city, and so successfully that within a few years of its foundation

---

[26] See *GV* 483. For the text of their vows, see *FN* 1:20–21. After pronouncing their vows they visited the other six churches. In 1606, giving his testimony prior to Ignatius' beatification, Pedro de Ribadeneira affirmed that he had accompanied them, had witnessed the vow ceremony, and later, after visiting Saint John Lateran, he had prepared a supper for them.

[27] For a description of Ignatius with reference to his appearance, speech, dress, and work, see *FX* 475–82.

the Society had houses in the major cities of Europe. From these fruitful contacts a continuous stream of candidates for the Society made its way to Rome, among them Peter Canisius[28] and Francis Borgia.[29] As Jesuit influence increased in these cities, colleges were opened, and so rapid was the Society's growth that by 1556, the year of Ignatius' death, it totaled one thousand members in seventy-six houses in twelve provinces, including Brazil, Japan, and India.

Ignatius began writing the Constitutions in 1541; though the process may have been slow, it was, nevertheless, thorough. By 1548 he saw himself nearing the end, and so he asked the professed fathers to come to Rome, and during

---

[28] Canisius, whose family name was Kanis, was born in Nijmegen, the Netherlands, on May 8, 1521. Having heard about the recently established Society of Jesus, he went to Mainz to search out Pierre Favre and to learn more about the Society. Favre led him through the Exercises and accepted him into the Society on May 8, 1543. After ordination to the priesthood, Canisius served as Cardinal Truchsess' *peritus* at the Council of Trent in 1547. He then taught in Sicily, from which task he was called to go to Germany and there worked at Ingolstadt, then in Vienna and Prague. He was appointed provincial of Germany in 1556 and held that office until 1569, when he retired to Innsbruck to spend his time writing. In 1580 he traveled to Fribourg, Switzerland, to establish a new college and remained there until his death on December 21, 1597. He was canonized by Pope Pius XI on May 31, 1925.

[29] Borgia was born on October 28, 1510, the oldest son of the third Duke of Gandía. He married Eleanor de Castro of Portugal in 1529, and his cousin, Emperor Charles V, made him Marquis of Lombay in 1530 and then Viceroy of Catalonia in 1539. Upon his father's death in December 1541, he succeeded to the duchy of Gandía. His first contact with a Jesuit was with Pierre Favre in 1542 or earlier. Subsequent to his wife's death, he expressed his desire to enter the Society, which he did on October 9, 1546, and he was permitted to take his vows while still administering his estates. He visited Ignatius in Rome (October 1550–February 1551), and upon his return to Spain he resigned his title in favor of his son Carlos. He was ordained to the priesthood on May 23, 1551, and upon the death of Diego Laínez, he was elected general of the Society on July 2, 1565. He died in Rome on September 30, 1572, and was canonized by Pope Clement X on April 12, 1671.

December 1550 and January 1551 he submitted the Constitutions to their scrutiny and asked for their observations. The fathers heartily approved what had been shown them, and Ignatius recognized that in places the text had to be clarified or expanded. Standing before these same fathers, Ignatius, on January 30, 1551, humbly asked to resign his office as general, citing his numerous sins, imperfections, and infirmities, which, in his judgment, prevented him from governing the Society as he felt it should be governed.[30] But the Jesuits gathered in Rome refused to accept the resignation and begged him, for the good of the Society, to continue bearing the burden of government.[31]

In 1551 Ignatius established the Roman College, which he wanted to be the model for all Jesuit colleges throughout the world.[32] To help counteract the growing influence of the Reformation in Germany, he established in 1552 a college in Rome for German seminarians so that they could be properly and thoroughly trained for the work that would be demanded of them on their return to their homeland. Ignatius was likewise attuned to the needs of Rome. He founded the House of Saint Martha for former prostitutes and a home for young girls who were especially in danger of being exploited, and he established an orphanage and had a house made ready for Muslims and Jews who had expressed a desire to become Christians.

---

[30] For the text of this resignation, see *LIL* 230.

[31] Of all the fathers present, only one, Andrés de Oviedo (1517–1577), felt that whatever Ignatius desired should be done. The others were unanimous in maintaining that they would have no other as general while Ignatius lived. Oviedo had earlier led Francis Borgia through the Exercises prior to the latter's entrance into the Society. Oviedo was later appointed to the Ethiopian mission, was ordained bishop in 1555, and became Patriarch of Ethiopia in 1562.

[32] For a history of the beginning and growth of the Roman College, see P. Caraman, *University of the Nations* (New York: Paulist, 1981).

Ever since his Paris days, Ignatius had suffered from stomach ailments; these were especially troublesome during the last ten years of his life. As his work increased, especially his concern about the Society's Constitutions, his health declined. There were months during 1554 and 1555 when he was unable to leave his sickbed. In the winter of 1555–1556 he found new strength, but by April he was again failing. The Roman summer of 1556 was oppressive, and since Ignatius was not improving his physician recommended that he go to the villa on the Aventine. This he did on July 2. The air there, however, was no more salubrious than that of the city, and so on July 26 or 27 he returned to the residence in the center of Rome. So intense was the heat that several Jesuits at the residence also fell ill with fever. When the physician came to examine these sick Jesuits, he also checked on Ignatius. The Founder was neither better nor worse, and since he had survived similar bouts in the past the physician felt certain that he would survive this one as well. Ignatius, however, thought differently.

On Thursday, July 30, Ignatius called his secretary, Polanco, to his bedside and asked him to go to the Vatican that afternoon to request the pope's blessing for him, to recommend the Society to his good will, and to assure him that if, by God's mercy, he were admitted into heaven, his prayer for the Vicar of Christ would be all the more fervent. Though Ignatius was suggesting that his death was imminent, Polanco put more trust in the physician's statement that he would recover. And so he informed Ignatius that since he had several letters that had to be written and sent to Spain that day, he would go to the Vatican on the following day. Ignatius intimated that he would prefer Polanco to go that afternoon; nevertheless, he told him: "Do as you wish." Polanco returned to his letters. Later, when Polanco was with Ignatius for the evening meal, they chatted as usual, and, certain that he had made the right decision, Polanco went peacefully to bed.[33]

Shortly after midnight, Ignatius took a turn for the worse. When the brother infirmarian checked on him at daybreak, it was clear that he was in his last moments. The brother hurriedly called several priests to the Founder's room, and Polanco rushed off to the Vatican to secure the papal blessing. But before he returned, Ignatius, the one-time soldier who had become a pilgrim for the love of Christ had given his soul to God.[34] The news of his death brought many to the Jesuit residence, and when the body was made ready for viewers, there was a line of cardinals and priests, of Rome's nobility and Rome's poor, all coming to kiss the venerable hands of the Founder of the Society of Jesus. On Saturday evening, August 1, he was buried[35] in the Church of Our Lady della Strada, and in 1587, when that edifice was replaced by the present church of the Gesú, his remains were interred there.

Ignatius of Loyola was beatified by Pope Paul V on July 27, 1609, and was canonized by Pope Gregory XV on March 12, 1622.

---

[33] For Polanco's account of Ignatius' death, see *GV* 1020.

[34] See Hugo Rahner, "The Death of Ignatius: 1536", in his *Ignatius: The Man and the Priest* (Rome: Centrum Ignatianum Spiritualitatis, 1997), 107–24.

[35] See *GV* 1022–24.

PREFACE OF
FATHER LUIS GONÇALVES DA CÂMARA

1. One Friday morning, August 4, the vigil of Our Lady of the Snows, in the year 1553, while the Father was in the garden near the house or apartment known as that of the duke, I began giving him an account of some matters pertaining to my soul, and I spoke to him, among other things, about vainglory. As a remedy the Father counseled me frequently to refer all my affairs to God, to aim at offering Him all the good that I find in myself, to acknowledge that these are all His gifts, and to thank Him for them. He spoke to me about these matters in such a way that I was greatly

1. Luis Gonçalves da Câmara[1] was a Portuguese Jesuit who had come to Rome in 1553, and had been minister (assistant to the superior) in the community where Ignatius lived. He held the Founder of the Society in such esteem that throughout this Preface he refers to Ignatius as "the Father". When he met with Ignatius in the garden near the duke's apartment—so-called because Francis Borgia, while still Duke of Gandía, stayed there on his visit to Rome during the Holy Year of 1550–1551—Ignatius was sixty-two years old and had but three more years to live. Because pilgrims going to the Holy Land were greatly respected and at times even regarded as saintly individuals, Ignatius deliberately kept reticent about his trip. He feared that if he were to reveal his plans, others would show him undeserved honor, and rather than expose himself to any temptation toward vanity he kept his projected pilgrimage a secret.

[1]Some details of his life have already been given in the first part of the Introduction.

consoled, and as a result I could not hold back my tears. The Father then told me how for two years he had struggled against this vice and with such effort that when he was about to set sail from Barcelona for Jerusalem he dared not tell anyone that he was going to Jerusalem, and he did the same in other circumstances. He added, with regard to this matter, that great peace of soul was his ever afterward.

An hour or two later we were at dinner, and while Master Polanco and I were eating with him, our Father said that many times Master Nadal and others of the Society had made a special request of him, but he had never come to any decision about it. Now, after having spoken with me, and hav-

Later that day at dinner, Ignatius mentioned that some members of the Society—and among these were Polanco[2] and Nadal[3]—had asked him to leave an account of the way God had worked in his soul, leading him to conversion and to the founding of the Society of Jesus. This request was first made of Ignatius in 1552,[4] but up to August 1553 he had done nothing about it. Now, after the day's conversation in the garden, he realized that if he were to narrate his life it would not be an exercise in vanity but an exercise in humility. He would not be relating his own accomplish-

---

[2] Juan Alfonso de Polanco was born in Burgos, Spain, on December 24, 1517, and entered the Society in Rome in 1541. He was named secretary of the Society in 1547 and held that position not only during Ignatius' lifetime, but also during the generalates of Diego Laínez and Francis Borgia. He died in Rome on December 20, 1576.

[3] Jerónimo Nadal was born on August 11, 1507, in Palma de Mallorca, attended the University of Paris at the same time that Ignatius was there, and entered the Society in Rome on November 23, 1545. From 1548–1551 he was in Sicily; he made his final profession in Rome on March 25, 1552, and was then sent to Spain as Commissar General. He returned to Rome in 1554, then traveled throughout Italy, Germany, and Spain, promulgating the Society's new Constitutions. He died in Rome on April 3, 1580.

[4] In Nadal's Preface to the Latin translation of Gonçalves da Câmara's text (see Appendix I), he says that he had made this request of Ignatius in 1551, but since he spent all of that year in Sicily, he must have meant 1552.

ing gone to his room, he felt a powerful inclination and desire to fulfill that request, and—speaking in such a way that it was clear that God had inspired him to see what his duty was—he was now determined to do it, that is, narrate all that had happened in his soul up to the present time, and he likewise decided that I was to be the one to whom he would reveal these matters.

2. At that time the Father was very ill and was not in the habit of promising himself even a single day more. In fact, whenever anyone said: "I'll do that two weeks hence", or "a week from today", the Father, somewhat surprised, always said: "What's that? Do you think you will live that long?"

ments but God's wondrous actions in him. If what he was about to tell Gonçalves da Câmara would prove helpful to him, perhaps the same would be helpful to others as well. Thus he decided to grant the request made of him.

2. Though Ignatius had come to the decision to narrate his life in early August 1553, Gonçalves da Câmara's Preface seems to indicate that the narration began in September of that year. Here he differs from what he says in no. 10 of the text, where he writes that that part was written in August 1553. Perhaps when writing his Preface he did not take the time to read what he had previously written and merely meant to say that the first portion was completed during September of that year. Altogether he had four or five meetings (August–September) with Ignatius before the first major interruption came. How much material was covered during those meetings? The Preface says that Ignatius got as far as his first days in Manresa and that the difference in the handwriting—where one scribe ended and another began—would indicate the place where the first meetings ended.

It would be helpful to pinpoint the exact place in the text where that interruption occurred, but since the original manuscript has been lost and only copies remain, there is no way of examining the difference in scribal penmanship. The mention of Ignatius' first days in Manresa, however, is a help. Since Ignatius experienced his singular illumination on the banks of the Cardoner River some months after his arrival in Manresa (nos. 30–31), it would then seem that the first talks ended somewhere between no. 19 and no. 30.

Nevertheless, on this occasion, he said that he hoped to live for three or four months so that he could complete this task. In speaking to him the following day I asked when he would like us to begin, and he replied that every day I should remind him of it (I cannot recall how many days!), until he felt ready to do so. Not having the time because of pressing duties, he wanted me to remind him of it every Sunday. Thus, in September (I do not remember the date), the Father called me and began to tell me about his entire life, as well as his youthful escapades, and all this clearly and distinctly and in full detail. Later in the same month he called me three or four times and carried his story up to his first days in Manresa, as one can see by the difference in the writing.

3. The Father's manner of narrating is the same he usually uses in everything else; he does it with such clarity that it seems that the whole past is made present to the listener. Thus, there was no need of my asking him any questions because whatever was essential to make the story intelligible the Father did not forget to relate. Without saying anything to the Father, I immediately went to write the points down, first sketchily and in my own hand, and later at greater length

During these meetings Ignatius likewise described the various escapades of his youth, and this was not a mere mention of them, for they were told with all their details. These capers, however, are not included in the text as it has come down to us. Were they in the original manuscript now lost? If so, were they deleted when copies were made? If not in the original manuscript, was it because Ignatius himself did not want them recorded, or was it the writer's decision to omit them?[5] It is because of this silence with regard to Ignatius' early life that the text begins in the year 1521, when he was thirty years old.

---

[5] *FN* 1:330–31 treats these questions and concludes that Gonçalves da Câmara chose not to include them.

as it is now written. I have tried not to write a single word other than those that I have heard from the Father, and with regard to those where I fear I have failed, it is because, not wanting to depart from the Father's words, I have not been able to explain properly the force of some of them. Thus, as I noted above, I was writing this up to September 1553, but from that time until Father Nadal arrived on October 18, 1554, the Father was continually giving excuses because of some illness or because various matters had to be attended to, telling me: "Remind me when this business is over." And when it was over and I reminded him, he said: "Right now, we are busy with another matter. Remind me when this is finished."

4. When Father Nadal arrived, he was very happy to see that the project was begun and told me to urge the Father to continue, telling me many times that the Father could do nothing better for the Society than this and that this was to give the Society's true foundations. He himself spoke to the Father many times, and the Father told me to jog his

---

4. By the time Nadal returned to Rome in October 1554, Ignatius' story had been interrupted for over a year, but he expressed his joy in hearing that the project he had requested had at last begun.[6] Then a series of affairs and events succeeded in prolonging the interruption. At one time it was the question of getting an endowment for the Roman College so that there would be no need to ask tuition of the students. Then it was the question of sending missionaries to Ethiopia. King John III of Portugal had been interested in bringing the Abyssinian Christians into the Catholic Church and had asked Ignatius to supply the missionaries. During

---

[6] Nadal, in his Preface, no. 3, says that upon his return from Spain he learned that nothing had been done on the project. Since Nadal wrote his Preface some six to eleven years after the event and seems not to have been aware of Gonçalves da Câmara's Preface, it is possible that his memory did not serve him well.

memory when the business of the college's endowment was completed. When that was over, then it was until the question of Prester John was settled and the courier had departed.

We began the story's continuation on March 9. Then Pope Julius III became critically ill and died on the twenty-third, and the Father put the matter off until there was a new pope, but it happened that he too soon fell ill and died. This was Marcellus. The Father postponed everything until the election of Pope Paul IV. Afterward, because of the heat and a great deal of business to attend to, he kept delaying until September 21, when the question arose about sending me to Spain. For this reason I strongly urged the Father to fulfill the promise he had made to me. So he made plans to meet me on the morning of the twenty-second in the Red Tower. After I had said Mass I went to him to ask if this was the time.

5. He answered that I should go and wait for him in the Red Tower and that I should be there when he arrived. I took it for granted that I would have to wait for him for

---

the Middle Ages, the king of the Abyssinians was believed to be the legendary Prester John.

Ignatius resumed his narration of March 9, 1555. It did not last long, however, because Pope Julius III succumbed on the twenty-third of that month, and Ignatius postponed the project until Marcello Cervini, who took the name Marcellus II, was elected on April 9. But that pope unexpectedly died on May 1. He was then succeeded by Pope Paul IV (Gian Pietro Carafa), elected on May 23. The interruption continued throughout the summer and was resumed only because Gonçalves da Câmara had been informed (September 21) that he would soon be leaving for Portugal. With his days in Rome numbered, he pressed Ignatius to continue his story, and thus they arranged to meet on the twenty-second in the Red Tower, a recently purchased building adjacent to the Society's residence.

5. Because of the writer's eagerness to read Ignatius' facial expressions, he seems to have approached so near that Ignatius asked him to observe the rule dealing with religious decorum that recommended that one should

some time, and so while I was in a hall talking to a brother, who had asked me a question, the Father came and reprimanded me for failing in obedience since I had not been waiting for him in the appointed place. That day he did not want to do anything. We then went to him and strongly urged him to continue. He returned to the Red Tower and dictated as he paced the floor, as he always did when dictating. I kept getting nearer and nearer to him so that I could better observe his facial expressions, but the Father said: "Observe the rule!" Forgetting this admonition, I again came near him, two or three times, and the Father repeated the admonition and went off. After some time he returned to the Tower to complete his dictation as we have it here written. Since I had, for some time been preparing to begin my

not stare fixedly at another's face but should keep his eyes slightly lowered.[7] It is not known how many meetings there were before the writer's departure on October 23. In the Preface he indicates that the last meeting took place on October 22, but according to no. 99 of the text, the final conversation took place on the twentieth. Because his departure was imminent, the writer could not record what he had received from Ignatius in any detail but had to be satisfied with a few notes reflecting the gist of the narration. After he had arrived in Genoa, and unable to find a scribe capable of writing Spanish, he settled for an Italian, and, thus, he fleshed out his notes in poor Italian, with the scribe dutifully setting them down. The general presumption is that the material received during the March 1555 meetings with Ignatius covered the Founder's life up to the beginning of no. 79 of the text, and was written in Spanish, while the final portion, written in Italian, reflects the material of September–October.

---

[7] The second rule of *The Rules of Decorum* reads as follows: "The eyes, for the most part, should be kept lowered and should not be immoderately raised or allowed to rove from side to side, and when conversing with persons to whom special deference is due, one should not regard him fixedly, but should keep the eyes slightly lowered" (*OC* 89 n. 13).

journey (the eve of my departure was the last day that the Father had spoken to me on these matters), I was unable to write anything out in detail while in Rome. Not having a Spanish scribe in Genoa, I dictated in Italian, from the notes that I had brought with me from Rome, and I put the finishing touches to this narration in the month of December 1555, in Genoa.

According to the Preface, the writer completed the text of Ignatius' narrative in December 1555, while in Genoa. He may have written the Preface while there or while on his way to Portugal, but it seems to have been written prior to Ignatius' death in 1556,[8] for he always refers to Ignatius in the present tense. If Ignatius had already died, one would have expected the writer to mention that fact in his Preface.[9]

---

[8] *FN* 1:330 indicates that there are some who think the Preface was written during the years 1558–1559, when Gonçalves da Câmara was in Rome attending the Society's first General Congregation or while acting as assistant to the new Father General Diego Laínez. In 1559 he returned to Portugal to be tutor to young King Sebastian.

[9] The extant Spanish manuscripts of this Preface lack no. 5 and abruptly end midpoint in the final sentence of no. 4. The text of no. 5 as given here is based on the Latin translation of Gonçalves da Câmara's text.

Chapter 1

Pamplona—Loyola
Convalescence and Conversion

(Mid-May 1521—Late February 1522)

1. Up to his twenty-sixth year he was a man given to worldly vanities, and having a vain and overpowering desire to gain renown, he found special delight in the exercise of arms. Thus he was in a fortress under attack by the French, and while everyone else clearly saw that they could not defend themselves and thought that they should surrender to save their lives, he offered so many reasons to the fortress'

---

1. In this narrative Ignatius twice mentions his age. Here he says that he was twenty-six when injured at Pamplona, and since that occurred in 1521, it would indicate that he was born in 1495. Later, however, he will state in no. 30 that in 1555 he was sixty-two years old, and that would then mean that he was born in 1493. This inconsistency has caused his biographers much anxiety. In the Introduction we have given 1491 as the probable date of Ignatius' birth, together with the reasons for choosing that date. Ignatius was, then, about thirty years old when he was wounded at Pamplona.

King Ferdinand the Catholic conquered the Kingdom of Navarre in 1512 and annexed it to Castile in 1515. To ensure Spanish control, the walls of Pamplona, the capital, were strengthened and a new fortress overlooking the walls constructed. Francis I of France, deciding to support Henri d'Albret's claim to Navarre, sent, in early 1521, a force to help regain it. The French force under André de Foix, Lord of Asparros, made

37

commander that he talked him into defending it. Though this was contrary to the opinion of all the other knights, still each drew encouragement from his firmness and fearlessness. When the day of the expected assault came, he made

its way through southern France, crossed the Pyrenees, entered Navarre, and headed toward Pamplona. The Duke of Nájera, Viceroy of Navarre, left a garrison of soldiers and artillery supplies in the Pamplona fortress, while he, on May 17, went to Segovia to seek from the Royal Council reinforcements against the French. By the time the duke arrived in Segovia, the French were but a mile from Pamplona. The duke had earlier sent word to Ignatius, who was then in Guipúzcoa, his native region, helping to quell a minor insurrection, to return to Pamplona. In response to the duke's urgent request, Ignatius enlisted the services of his elder brother, Martín García, together with men from the family's estate and the province, and hastened to keep the French from entering Pamplona.

Since there were many French sympathizers in Pamplona, these convinced the citizenry that it would be better to welcome the French than to have their city destroyed in a siege. When the two Loyola brothers and their forces arrived at the gates of Pamplona, they joined Pedro de Beaumont, leader of the Spanish garrison in the city, in trying to persuade the people to resist the French. They were unsuccessful, and seeing that the citizens were willing to capitulate to the French, Martín García turned his back on Pamplona and returned home. Ignatius remained, but when he learned that Pedro de Beaumont likewise favored surrender, he took his men and rode to the fortress.

Since the city had decided to greet the French with open arms, Miguel de Herrera, commander of the fortress, felt that any defense on his part would be futile. The fortress would be attacked from all sides, and since his men were too few in number to withstand a prolonged siege, he too spoke of surrender. Ignatius was of another opinion, and he offered reasons why they should stand their ground and fight. These reasons have not been preserved, but surely one was that it would be shameful to surrender before battle had begun. On May 19 Pamplona sent word to André de Foix that the city was his. The French entered that day and immediately set up their artillery and directed it against the fortress. These preparations were observed by Ignatius and the garrison, and thus they expected the assault to begin that very day. Since Ignatius intended to fight to his last breath, and because there was no chaplain among them, he asked one his confession to one of his comrades in arms. After the attack had lasted a good while, a cannonball hit him in a leg, shattering it completely, and since the ball passed between both legs the other one was likewise severely wounded.

of his comrades to hear his confession. In this he followed the custom of his time, namely, if in danger of death and no priest is available, to confess one's sins to a lay person. Such a confession was never considered sacramental, but it clearly manifested the individual's contrition for sin.[1]

Ignatius says nothing about the length of the siege, nor does he give the date of his injury. From his statement the reader can easily conclude that the wounding took place some time after the heavy bombardment had begun, probably on the second day of the attack, with surrender several hours later. This, in fact, has been the traditional interpretation of his statement, that is, the siege beginning on May 19 (Pentecost Sunday) and the wounding on the twentieth (Pentecost Monday).[2] However, documents describing this siege have recently been discovered, and according to these, light shelling began on May 19, and it was only on the twenty-third that the heavy artillery (for example, culverins, cannons) was brought into place. The fortress surrendered on May 23 or 24.[3] Since Ignatius' right leg had been shattered by a small-sized ball that entered through a portion of the wall that had crumbled, the injury could have taken place during a period of heavy bombardment, that is, either on May 23 or May 24.

---

[1] Saint Thomas Aquinas allows this practice (*Summa theologiae. Supplementum*, quest. 8, art. 2, resp.), and the prayer books of the fifteenth and sixteenth centuries approved the custom.

[2] It appears that Nicholas Orlandini, S. J., was the first to indicate May 20 as the date of Ignatius' injury, namely, "xiii Kal. Junii", in his *Historia Societatis Iesu* (Rome, 1614), bk. 1, p. 4.

[3] For a detailed description of the events in Pamplona, prior to and after Ignatius' injury, as well as the suggestion that the wounding may have taken place on May 23, see Luis Fernández Martín, "Iñigo López de Loyola y el proceso contra Miguel de Herrera, alcaide de la fortaleza de Pamplona", in his *Los años juveniles de Iñigo de Loyola: Su formación en Castilla* (Valladolid: Caja de Ahorros Popular de Valladolid, 1981), 283–351. If Ignatius was wounded on May 20, as tradition maintains, then he remained with little or no medical attention until the fortress surrendered three days later. His account (no. 2), however, seems to indicate that surrender came shortly after his wounding.

2. As soon as he fell wounded the others in the fortress surrendered to the French, who, after they had gained control, treated the wounded man very well, showing him courtesy and kindness. After being in Pamplona some twelve or fifteen days, they transported him on a litter to his home country. His condition was serious, and the physicians and surgeons, summoned from many places, agreed that the leg should be broken again and the bones reset, since they either

2. With Ignatius now wounded, the other knights and soldiers lost courage and shortly thereafter surrendered the fortress to the French. Ignatius was taken into the city where French army surgeons set his leg and cared for his wounds. So kind were the French soldiers toward him that as a gesture of his appreciation Ignatius gave his shield to one of them, his dagger to another, and his cuirass to a third.[4] No trace of that Pamplona fortress remains today, but a church stands on the site dedicated to the one who was wounded there. Ignatius does not explicitly state who transported him to Loyola Castle, and the "they" in the text was traditionally interpreted to mean the French.[5] Recent research, however, has shown that Ignatius' compatriots, under the leadership of Esteban de Zuasti, a relative of Francis Xavier, undertook the task.[6] They placed the injured Ignatius on a litter and left Pamplona between June 2 and 5. After passing through valleys and crossing mountains, and a stopover at Anzuola,[7] where Ignatius' sister Magdalena resided,[8] the weary caravan arrived at Loyola about June 20.

Loyola Castle is situated between the towns of Azpeitia and Azcoitia, in the Basque province of Guipúzcoa, but when the wounded Ignatius returned in 1521, the castle was surrounded by woods and somewhat isolated from the towns. After his father's death in 1507, and that of Ignatius'

---

[4] See FN 1:156.

[5] Polanco states this in FN 1:157, and this has been the constant tradition among Jesuits.

[6] See GV 153.

[7] See GV 154.

[8] IdL 75 identifies this Magdalena as Ignatius' sister, while PY 63 n. 1 calls her his sister-in-law.

had been poorly set in the first place or had become dislocated during the journey, for they were now out of joint and would never heal. The butchery was repeated, and during it, as in other such operations that he had undergone before and would later undergo, he never uttered a word, nor did he show any sign of pain other than clenching his fists.

3. His condition grew much worse: he was unable to eat, and, in addition, he had the usual signs indicating the approach of death. On Saint John's feast the physicians, not expecting him to pull through, advised him to make his confession. He received the sacraments, and on the vigil of the

---

eldest brother, Juan Pérez, in 1496, during the Spanish campaign against Naples, the Master of Loyola was his elder brother Martín García. Martín had married Magdalena de Araoz, one of Queen Isabella's ladies-in-waiting, in 1498, and brought her home to Loyola. At that time Ignatius was but a child of seven. Since Martín was now engaged in fighting the French at Logroño, it was Magdalena who welcomed Ignatius to the ancestral home and cared for him while the bone in his leg was reset.

3. Ignatius was not home a week when his health so deteriorated that his physician despaired of his life. On June 24, the feast of Saint John the Baptist, he received the last sacraments, but then at midnight, June 28, as the vigil of Saints Peter and Paul was ending and the feast beginning, Ignatius' health unexpectedly turned for the better. Saint John the Baptist and Saint Peter were two of Ignatius' patrons: the former was the patron of the Oñaz side of the family, and the latter the patron of the Loyola side.[9] Both feasts were duly celebrated at the castle, and by noting that

---

[9] See *FN* 2:517; *IL* 40–41. While at Arévalo Ignatius is said to have written a poem in honor of Saint Peter. Next to the Arévalo castle was a church dedicated to the saint, and both were connected by a subterranean passage (see *MR* 12). Ignatius' verses in praise of Saint Peter have not survived, and A. Astrain wonders about the quality of those verses, since Ignatius had difficulty writing even prose (*Historia de la Compañía de Jesús en la Asistencia de España*, vol. 1, *San Ignacio de Loyola 1540-1556* [Madrid: Sucesores de Rivadeneyra, 1902], 18). Hugo Rahner refers to these verses as an "epic" (*The Spirituality of St. Ignatius Loyola* [Chicago: Loyola University, 1980], 20).

feast of Saints Peter and Paul the physicians informed him that if he did not feel better by midnight he could count himself a dead man. Now, the sick man was devoted to Saint Peter, and our Lord thus desired that his recovery begin that very midnight. His improvement progressed so well that after a few days he was pronounced to be out of danger of death.

4. When the bones did knit together, the one below the knee rested on top of the other so that the leg was shortened and the bone so protruded that it made an unsightly bump. Because he was determined to make a way for himself in the world, he could not tolerate such ugliness and thought it marred his appearance. Thus he instructed the surgeons to remove it, if possible. They told him that it could certainly be sawn away, but the pain would be greater than any he had suffered up to now, since the leg had healed and it would take some time to remove the bump. Nevertheless, he was determined to endure this martyrdom to satisfy his personal

---

these events took place on the feast of his patrons, Ignatius was indicating that he saw God's special intervention in his recovery.[10]

4. Good news came to Loyola in early July. The French were finally defeated at Noaín on June 30, in which battle Martín García had participated. All Navarre was again under Spanish control, and the nation's flag was once more flying over the fortress in Pamplona. It was a happy Martín García who returned to find his brother recuperating on the castle's third floor, and as he narrated the events that led to the French defeat, perhaps Ignatius thought his wound was worth it.

Ignatius still burned with the desire for worldly renown, but with one leg shorter than the other, and with an ugly bone protruding, how could

---

[10] Some authors in the past have maintained that at the time of Ignatius' cure Saint Peter appeared to him, but none of the first companions speaks of such an appearance. It seems that Pedro de Ribadeneira was the first to mention it in his Spanish life of the Founder: "Thus it is understood that the glorious apostle appeared to him that very night" (FN 4:85).

taste. His older brother was horrified and said that he himself would not dare undergo such pain, but the wounded man suffered it with his accustomed patience.

5. After the flesh and the excess bone had been cut away, they tried to keep the leg from being too short by applying many ointments and by using mechanical devices to keep it

---

he wear the close-fitting boots then in fashion? How could he project a dashing knightly image if he had a limp? There was but one answer—the offending bone would have to be cut away. While his brother recoiled at the thought of such an operation, Ignatius was determined to have it done so that he could continue his career in the world, and for that world he was willing to endure a martyrdom.

5. Ignatius had not only submitted to an excruciating operation but likewise to a systematic stretching of his leg that meant weeks of pain and immobility.[11] By the end of August, or perhaps in early September, he felt sufficiently recovered to seek distraction, and, thus, he asked his sister-in-law if she had any chivalrous romances, his favorite type of reading. Novels dealing with knightly exploits were the best-sellers of the sixteenth century. The most famous of these was *Amadís de Gaula*, which Ignatius acknowledges to have read (no. 17). A Castilian edition appeared in 1508 and was followed by a sequel and many imitations, many of them poor in quality. The titles of the other novels that Ignatius might have read at Arévalo are unknown to us, but he spent many an hour reading them while serving the Duke of Nájera.[12]

---

[11] From Martín García's will we learn that the surgeon who operated on Ignatius and cared for him was Martín de Iztiola and that he had been paid ten ducats for his services. See *FN* 1:369 n. 9 or *FD*, doc. 116.

[12] Since Ignatius read *Amadís*, he must also have read its sequel, *The Deeds of Esplandián* (Esplandián was Amadís' son), and there were other novels and other heroes. During the first quarter of the sixteenth century, Spain produced some twenty-nine such novels. So popular were they that parents named their children after these legendary heroes: Tristan, Florestan, Presebal. Ignatius not only read these novels, but he also imitated their heroes. Polanco says: "Though he was ever loyal to the faith, he did not live in conformity with it, nor did he preserve himself from sin. Especially did he indulge in gaming, duelling, and affairs with women" (*IdL* 42–43).

continually stretched. For many a day he had to endure this martyrdom. But our Lord restored his health, and he grew better. He was healthy in every respect except that he could not readily stand on that leg, and he was thus forced to remain in bed. Since he was an avid reader of books of worldly fiction, commonly called chivalrous romances, and since he

Since such novels were unknown in the Loyola household, Magdalena offered him the only books she had. These were not exactly what Ignatius had requested, but they would help him pass the time of day. She offered him the four volumes of Ludolph of Saxony's *The Life of Jesus Christ,* which she had received as a gift from Queen Isabella. Ludolph—who was born in Strasbourg in 1295 and died there in 1377—was a Carthusian monk, and his work, written in Latin, had been translated into Castilian by Ambrosio de Montesino, O.F.M., at the request of King Ferdinand and Queen Isabella. It was printed in Alcalá in 1502–1503. Ludolph's book was the first formal life of our Lord to appear in print, and it was an exceptional blend of Scripture and the piety of the Middle Ages.[13] The other book that Magdalena gave him was the popular *Golden Legend* of Jacobus de Voragine—who was born in Varazze about 1226, entered the Dominicans, and died in 1298 as Archbishop of Genoa.[14] This book was

---

[13] While Ignatius merely mentions that a life of Christ was given him, Nadal identifies it as that of Ludolph of Saxony (see *FN* 2:186). The book's full title is *Vita Jesu Christi e quatuor evangeliis et scriptoribus orthodoxis concinnata per Ludolphum de Saxonia.* Ludolph entered the Carthusians in 1340, after having been a Dominican. He presumably switched because of a desire for a more contemplative form of life. After being prior of various monasteries, he ended his days in Strasbourg. It is not known when he wrote his book, but it seems certain that it was during his days as a Carthusian, for he quotes many Carthusian authors.

[14] Nadal informs us that the book containing the lives of the saints was *Flos sanctorum* (*FN* 2:187). The book's actual title is *Legenda aurea.* The author, Giacomo da Varazze (latinized to Jacobus de Voragine), became a Dominican in 1244 and rose to be provincial of his region. He was elected Archbishop of Genoa in 1288, but he declined the honor. He was again elected in 1292, and this time he had to yield to the will of Pope Nicholas IV. He died six years later. The *Legenda aurea* was written between 1253 and 1270.

was feeling quite well, he asked for some such books to pass the time. In that house, however, they found none of the type he was used to reading, and so they brought him *The Life of Christ* and a book on the lives of the saints in Spanish.

6. By frequent reading of these books he grew somewhat fond of what he found written therein. Setting his reading aside, he sometimes paused to think about the things he had read, and at other times he thought of the worldly things that had formerly occupied his mind. Of the many idle things that came to him, one took such a hold on his heart that, without his realizing it, it engrossed him for two or three hours at a time. He dreamed what he would achieve in the service of a certain lady and thought of the means he would take to go to the land where she lived, the clever

more popularly known as *Flos sanctorum*, because it contained brief lives of the saints. The translator of the Castilian version is anonymous, but the book had been in circulation in Spain since 1480. The edition that Ignatius most probably used was by the Cistercian Gauberto Maria Vagad, which first appeared in 1493 and was reprinted at Toledo in 1511. These volumes were Ignatius' sole reading during his months of convalescence.

6. Ignatius read and reread passages from *The Life of Jesus Christ* and the lives of the saints in the *Golden Legend*. After a period of reading, he usually paused to reflect on whatever had touched him. Though his reading found a definite response in his heart, he still found himself, at times, thinking that he was another Amadís performing heroic deeds for his lady. This lady of Ignatius' dreams has always remained elusive. Since she was higher in station than a countess or a duchess, she must have been a member of the royal family.

Three ladies have been suggested by Ignatius' various biographers. (1) It has been proposed that the lady in question may have been Queen Germaine de Foix,[15] niece of Louis XII of France and second wife of

---

[15] See *IL* 43.

sayings and words he would speak to her, and the knightly deeds he would perform for her. He was so enraptured with these thoughts that he never considered how impossible it was for him to accomplish them, for the lady was not one of the lesser nobility; neither was she a countess, or a duchess, but her station was much higher than any of these.

Ferdinand the Catholic. When Ferdinand died in 1516, Germaine was in her late twenties. In 1519 she married the Margrave of Brandenburg and was still married to him at the time of Ignatius' daydreams. (2) Another candidate is the Infanta Catalina,[16] the youngest sister of Emperor Charles V. She was born in 1507 but spent her entire youth in the gloomy surroundings of the royal palace at Tordesillas, where her mother, the mad Queen Juana, was detained. When Charles convened the Cortes at Valladolid in February 1518, to receive the allegiance of the nobility, he brought Catalina to the city to present (March 13) her to his court. She was only eleven, but contemporary accounts describe her as being most beautiful. Since Ignatius' new master, the Duke of Nájera, was present on that occasion, it can be presumed that Ignatius was likewise there and had his first glimpse of the royal princess. In 1524 Catalina married John III of Portugal, and after the Society of Jesus had been founded, John III proved to be one of the most loyal friends the Jesuits had ever known.[17] (3) The final candidate is Leonor,[18] elder sister of Emperor Charles and Catalina, who was married to Manuel, King of Portugal, at the time of Ignatius' convalescence.

Was the lady of Ignatius' thoughts one of these three, or another? Ignatius chose to be silent on this point, and it is likely that her identity will always elude us.

---

[16] See Pedro Leturia, S.J., "Notas críticas sobre la dama del Capitán Loyola", *Archivum Historicum Societatis Iesu* 5 (1936): 84–92.

[17] With reference to the queen's interest in the Society in Portugal, as well for Ignatius' letter to her and the relics she requested, see *LW* 45–51.

[18] See Felix de Llanos y Torriglia, "El Capitán Iñigo de Loyola y la dama de sus pensamientos", *Razón y Fe* 124 (1941): 33–69.

7. Our Lord, nevertheless, came to his aid, bringing it about that these thoughts were followed by others arising from his reading. While reading the life of our Lord and those of the saints, he used to pause and meditate, reasoning with himself: "What if I were to do what Saint Francis did, or to do what Saint Dominic did?" Thus in his thoughts he dwelt on many good deeds, always suggesting to himself great and difficult ones, but as soon as he considered doing them, they all appeared easy of performance. Throughout these thoughts he used to say to himself: "Saint Dominic did this, so I have to do it too. Saint Francis did this, so I have to do it too." These thoughts lasted a long time, but after other thoughts had taken their place, the above-mentioned worldly ones returned to him, and he dwelt on them for quite some length. This succession of such diverse thoughts—of worldly exploits that he desired to accomplish, or those of God that came to his imagination—stayed with him for a long time as he turned them over in his mind, and when he grew weary of them he set them aside to think of other matters.

7. The reading that Ignatius did during his convalescence was, up to that time, the most important he had ever done, for it was through that reading that God began to act on his soul and draw him to a conversion of life. Ignatius was familiar with the Dominican and Franciscan orders, for they were not only the two most popular orders in the sixteenth century, but each had convents in the various cities and towns of Spain. There even was a Franciscan convent in Azpeitia, one of whose foundresses was his relative Maria López de Emparán y Loyola.[19] It is not surprising, then, that Ignatius should want to dwell on the lives of Saint Dominic and Saint Francis, but what is noteworthy is that he did not merely conclude that their lives were imitable but that he saw himself obliged to imitate them— that he, too, had to accomplish for God what they had accomplished.

---

[19] See *IdL* 13.

8. There was this difference, however. When he thought of worldly matters, he found much delight; but after growing weary and dismissing them, he found that he was dry and unhappy. But when he thought of going barefoot to Jerusalem and eating nothing but herbs and of imitating the saints in all the austerities they practiced, he not only found consolation in these thoughts, but even after they had left him he remained happy and joyful. He did not consider nor did he stop to examine this difference until one day his eyes were partially opened, and he began to wonder at this difference and to reflect upon it. From experience he knew that some thoughts left him sad while others made him happy, and little by little he came to perceive the different spirits that were moving him; one coming from the devil, the other coming from God.

9. He gained not a little light from this lesson, and he began to think more seriously about his past life and how greatly he needed to do penance for it. It was at this time that the desire to imitate the saints came to him, and without giving any consideration to his present circumstances,

8-9. Because of the various movements that he experienced in his soul during his months of convalescence, Ignatius eventually learned how to discern the spirits moving him. He came to realize that thoughts about the world left him dry and unhappy, while thoughts of a pilgrimage to Jerusalem and of penance brought him happiness and joy. He concluded that the former came from the devil, while the latter from God. Chief among the thoughts that produced joy was the idea of going to Jerusalem, and this desire most surely had its origin in his reading of Ludolph's life of Christ. The Proemium to that book, written by a Dominican of the thirteenth century and appropriated by Ludolph to serve as his introduction, speaks of the delight that fills one's heart when visiting the Holy Land. What joy to see the places where our Lord visited and to reflect that it was in those very places that our Lord worked our salvation! Ignatius' vivid imagination transported him to Jerusalem, and once that desire had taken he promised to do, with God's grace, what they had done. His greatest desire, after regaining his health, was to go to Jerusalem, as previously stated, and to observe the fasts and make use of the discipline as any generous soul on fire with God is accustomed to do.

10. With these holy desires of his, the thoughts of his former life were soon forgotten, and this was confirmed by a vision in this manner. One night, as he lay sleepless, he clearly saw the likeness of our Lady with the holy Child Jesus, and because of this vision he enjoyed an excess of consolation for a remarkably long time. He felt so great a loathsomeness for all his past life, especially for the deeds of the flesh, that it seemed to him that all the images that had been previously imprinted on his mind were now erased. Thus from that hour until August 1553, when this is being written, he never again consented, not even in the least matter, to the motions of the flesh. Because of this effect in him he concluded that this had been God's doing, though he did not dare to specify it any further or say anything more than to affirm what he

hold of his heart, he would not rest until it had been fulfilled. In addition, he intended to keep to a strict vegetarian diet and to adopt the austerities practiced by the saints, whose lives he had read in the *Golden Legend*.

10. Now that Ignatius had set aside the worldly thoughts that had once attracted him and decided to follow Christ after the example of His saints, his decision received divine confirmation. Ignatius simply relates that one evening, unable to fall asleep, he saw "the likeness of our Lady with the holy Child Jesus". He does not indicate whether he saw her with his bodily eyes, or whether it was with the eyes of his mind, that is, an interior experience. Nor does he indicate if our Lady spoke to him. What is clear is that he experienced her presence and that it had the remarkable result that from that moment onward he was filled with a total disgust for his former way of life. Through this signal grace Ignatius saw himself as one transformed. His former self now yielded to the true follower of Christ. Ignatius never revealed the date when this wondrous grace had come to

had said above. His brother interpreted his external change, as did other members of the household, to mean that an interior change had taken place in his soul.

11. Free of all cares, he continued his reading and his good resolves. During the time he spent talking to the members of the household, he spoke about the things of God, and he thus brought much profit to their souls. He greatly enjoyed his books, and the idea struck him to copy down, in abridged form, the more important items in the life of Christ and of the saints. Now that he began to get out of bed and move around the house a little, he set about writing these things in a book, taking great care and using red ink for Christ's words and blue for those of our Lady. He used polished and lined paper and wrote in a good hand since he had an attractive penmanship. He spent some of his time in writing and some in prayer. The greatest consolation he received at this time was from gazing at the sky and stars, and this he often did

him; August 15, 1521, has been suggested,[20] but it could well have been later, perhaps in September. This change in Ignatius did not go unnoticed. His brother observed that he was no longer the soldier he once had been, and his conversation was no longer about wars and knights but of God and His saints. Ignatius' conversion to God was now in progress, and the power of that vision remained with him to the end of his life.

11. God was now the focal point of Ignatius' life, and his entire day was spent in prayer, reading, and writing. Because he wanted to preserve some of the thoughts he found in his books, he decided to jot them down for future use. He took an account book—it was quarto in size and had three hundred pages—and in it he wrote our Lord's words in red ink, just as he had seen them in Ludolph's life of Christ, but it was his own idea to record those of our Lady in blue. This book, unfortunately, must have been lost at an early date, as none of Ignatius' first companions appears to have seen it. All they knew about it was its size and how many pages it

---

[20] See *IL* 45.

and for quite a long time. The result of all this was that he felt within himself a strong impulse to serve our Lord. He spent much time reflecting on his resolution and wished to be fully recovered so that he could set out on his journey.

12. Mulling over his plans and thinking of what he would do after he had returned from Jerusalem, so that he could live a life of constant penance, he thought of entering the Carthusian monastery in Seville, where he would not reveal his identity—so that they would not think much of him— and where his diet would be only herbs. But when he again thought of the penances he wanted to fulfill as he went about the world, his desire for the Carthusian way of life cooled, since he feared that there he would not be able to give vent to the hatred that he had conceived against himself.

had.[21] Now being able to move about the house and grounds, Ignatius took to gazing at the stars, a practice that stayed with him. Off the rooms he occupied in Rome as Father General, there is a small balcony, and there of an evening Ignatius frequently stood to look upon the Roman sky. As his health steadily improved, so grew his eagerness to begin his pilgrimage.

12. Ignatius was determined to go to the Holy Land, but what would he do when he returned home? His first thought was to enter the famous monastery of Nuestra Señora de las Cuevas on the outskirts of Seville. The buildings of the monastery still stand today but have not housed monks since the early part of the nineteenth century, when the monastery was secularized.[22] Ignatius' choice of the Carthusians undoubtedly came from the fact that Ludolph had been a Carthusian as well as because the order

---

[21] *PY* 69–70, n. 2.

[22] In 1836 the Spanish government sold the monastery buildings to the Pickman Pottery Works, and the factory remained there until 1982, when it moved to another location. The Spanish government subsequently acquired the property and, because of its historical importance to that area, restored portions of the original Charterhouse. See James Hogg, *La Cartuja de las Cuevas* (Salzburg: Institut für Anglistik und Americanistik, 1983).

Nevertheless, when a house servant was going to Burgos, he asked him to gather information about the Carthusian rule, and the information he received seemed satisfactory.

Because of the above-mentioned reason and because his mind was fully taken up with the journey that he was thinking of soon making, and since entering the monastery was something that could wait until his return, he did not think much more about it. Feeling that his strength had sufficiently returned, he judged it was time to depart, and he told his brother: "You are aware, my Lord, that the Duke of Nájera knows that I am again well.

had a reputation for being the most penitential in the Church. There Ignatius would be able to live the life of penance he so desired and to observe their rule of doing without meat. Because Seville was in southern Spain, hundreds of miles from Guipúzcoa, Ignatius felt that he would be unknown there, and, thus, in complete anonymity he could give himself to God.[23] A doubt, however, then came to mind: Perhaps the rules of the order would not permit him to live as severe a life as he would like. In that case he would live in the world, but he would a live a life of penance.

---

[23] How did Ignatius come to know of the Charterhouse in Seville? It has been suggested that, while at Nájera, Ignatius read Juan de Padilla's *Los doce triunfos de los doce Apóstoles* (1518), in which he describes his monastery of Our Lady of the Caves (e.g., *IdL* 41 and H. Rahner, *The Spirituality of St. Ignatius of Loyola* [Chicago: Loyola University, 1980], 20). This same work is sometimes mentioned as the inspiration for the verses that Ignatius dedicated to Saint Peter. However, neither Ignatius nor any of his first companions mentions his reading of Juan de Padilla's poetry. Perhaps, as suggested by Borja de Medina, Ignatius came to know of Our Lady of the Caves because he may have twice visited Seville. King Ferdinand had been there in 1508 and 1511, and it is most probable that the royal treasurer, Velázquez, was likewise there with his retinue, which included Ignatius. In no. 53 Ignatius explicitly states that he had met Rodrigo Portuondo "when the pilgrim served at the court of the Catholic King". Portuondo was, in fact, in Seville in 1511 because Ferdinand was then laying plans for an African campaign. See F. de Borja de Medina, "Íñigo López de Loyola: Probable estancia en Sevilla (1508 y 1511) y su reflejo en los Ejercicios", *Archivum Historicum Societatis Iesu* 63 (1994): 3–75, especially 20–29.

It would be good for me to go to Navarrete." (The duke was residing there at the time.) His brother led him from room to room and with much love for him pleaded with him not to throw his life away, but to acknowledge the great hopes people had placed in him and to see what he could make of himself. These and other similar arguments were all directed to dissuade him from his good desire, but without departing from the truth, for he was now very scrupulous about that, he answered in a way that enabled him to leave his brother.

Ignatius had not totally given up on the Carthusians, for when he learned that one of his brother's servants was going to Burgos, some sixty miles south of Loyola, he asked him to get some information about the Carthusian rule. The monastery there was La Real Cartuja de Miraflores. This had originally been a royal hunting lodge, but in 1442 it had been offered to the Carthusians, who still maintain it as a monastery. When Ignatius was enjoying *Amadís de Gaula*, he had read that it was to Miraflores that King Lisuarte and his wife retired after they abdicated the English throne in favor of Amadís and his wife, Oriana.

In Ignatius' plans, Jerusalem came before the monastery, and now that he felt strong enough to travel he did not want to postpone his departure any longer. Knowing how his brother would react if he had been told his plans in full, Ignatius merely informed him that it was time for him to visit the Duke of Nájera, who was then at Navarrete. Martín García sensed that Ignatius was not just going to visit the duke, and so before Ignatius departed, both brothers took a stroll through the family castle, visiting room after room. They recalled all who had lived there, their parents as well as their brothers who had died in battle. They spoke of the important events in their family's history and its proud heritage in the service of the kings of Castile. Martín García endeavored to show Ignatius that he had a bright military career before him and that the Loyola name was greatly honored and respected in northern Spain. Still, the brother's persuasion did not have its hoped-for result, for Ignatius was as determined as ever to dedicate himself to God. To be a knight in the service of an earthly king was now something in his past. Ignatius looked forward to being a knight in the service of an eternal King. It was late February 1522.

Chapter 2

Montserrat: A Knight's Vigil

(Late February–March 25, 1522)

13. As he mounted his mule, another brother of his wanted to travel with him as far as Oñate, and on the way he persuaded him to keep a vigil at the shrine of Our Lady of Aránzazu. That night he prayed for additional strength for his journey. He then left his brother in Oñate at the home of one of their sisters, whom his brother was going to visit, and

13. Hearing that Ignatius was about to leave for Navarrete, Pero López, Ignatius' priest-brother, asked to travel with him as far as Oñate, where he intended to visit their sister. Pero López had been Ignatius' companion in the carnival excesses in 1515. Since about 1518 Pero López had been pastor of the church of San Sebastián de Soreasu in Azpeitia.[1] Dressed as befitted his rank, with sword at his side, and accompanied by two attendants, Ignatius and his brother left Loyola Castle and headed southward to the shrine of Our Lady of Aránzazu. At the time of Ignatius' visit, the shrine was only fifty years old and had been built on the site where a Basque shepherd boy had found a statue of our Lady nestled in a thorny bush.[2] During his vigil there Ignatius placed his journey to Jerusalem under our Lady's care and asked heaven for the health and strength needed to

---

[1] *FD* 786.

[2] Tradition has it that on June 11, 1468, the young shepherd, Rodrigo de Balzategui, found the statue caught amid thorns and in amazement asked: "Aránzazu?" That is: "Are you under the thorns?" See *MR* 28.

went on toward Navarrete. Remembering that the duke's household owed him some ducats, he thought it a good time to collect them, and so he penned a note to the treasurer, who responded that he was short of funds. But when the duke heard this, he said that he could owe money to everyone else, but he must pay his debts to Loyola. The duke wanted to offer him—in recognition for what he had accomplished in the past—a position of authority, if he would accept it. He collected his money and ordered that it be divided among certain individuals to whom he felt some obligation and that a part of it be used for a statue of our Lady

fulfill his pilgrimage, as well as for the moral strength to continue in the good resolves he had made during his convalescence. It was most probably at Aránzazu that Ignatius made a vow of chastity. In later years he acknowledged that he had made such a vow during his journey from Loyola to Montserrat, but he never divulged the name of the place where he had made it. His biographers think that the shrine of Aránzazu would have been a suitable place for such a vow.[3]

After a night of prayer the brothers and servants headed northwest to Oñate, where Ignatius left Pero López with their sister. It is unclear which sister was then in Oñate, but it is presumed that it was Magdalena, who had recently married Juan López de Gallaiztegui in Anzuola and who was now visiting the Araoz family.[4] Taking leave of his brother and sister, Ignatius directed his mule toward Navarrete. Since the duke was then visiting Nájera, Ignatius submitted his bill, for services rendered in 1521, to the duke's treasurer. Since the duke had recently lost favor with his sovereign and had been replaced as viceroy in Navarre, his treasury may have been somewhat strained. Hearing that Ignatius was in Navarrete, the duke sent word that he was to be paid what was owed him, and, in addition, he offered him an important position, but Ignatius declined it. He spent part of the money he received settling unpaid debts, and the remainder was to

---

[3] See J. Iriarte, "Fijando el voto de castidad de S. Ignacio de Loyola", *Manresa* 3 (1927): 156–64.

[4] See *OC* 98 n. 3.

that was poorly decorated and which he wanted to be more appropriately appointed and ornamented. Saying good-bye to the two servants who traveled with him, he departed Navarrete, and, riding his mule, he headed for Montserrat.

14. Something happened as he was on his way, and it will be good to record it so that others may understand how our Lord dealt with that soul, still blind but filled with ardent desires to follow Him in every way he knew. Thus he decided to practice great penances, not with the view of satisfying for his sins, but to please and appease God. Whenever he made up his mind to do a certain penance that the saints had done, he was determined not only to do the same, but even more. All his consolation derived from these thoughts; he never considered anything about the interior life, nor did he know what humility was, or charity, or patience, or that

be used to refurbish an image of our Lady, perhaps in the church of Navarrete itself or at a nearby shrine.[5] Having settled his accounts, Ignatius sent the two servants back to Loyola and made his way alone to Montserrat.[6]

14. Looking back on himself, after some thirty years, and on the way he had first expressed his fervor, Ignatius acknowledged that he had been at that time still blind and uneducated in the spiritual life. To be sure, he desired to follow Christ, and to do this he chose to imitate the saints he had met in his reading during his months of convalescence. Whatever penances they had practiced, those he would also perform. The saints had likewise subjected their bodies to the discipline, even to the drawing of blood, and he would do the same. Now that he had left his home behind

---

[5] The original text (*imagen*) is unclear; it is not known whether this was a statue or a picture of our Lady. *IdL* 135 considers it a statue, while *IL* 52 speaks of it as a picture.

[6] Was Montserrat in Ignatius' thoughts when he left Loyola? He first mentions the shrine in no. 13, after his visit to Aránzazu. Perhaps it was his vigil at this tiny local shrine that gave him the idea of a more solemn night's vigil at the more famous shrine. Montserrat was on the road to Barcelona, so it would not have taken him out of his way.

discretion was the rule and measure of these virtues. His only intention, not having any other reason in mind, was to perform these important external actions because the saints had performed them for the glory of God.

15. As he continued his way, a Moor riding on a mule caught up with him, and in their conversation they began to speak about our Lady. The Moor said that it certainly seemed to him that the Virgin had conceived without the aid of man, but he could not believe that in giving birth she remained a virgin. To substantiate his opinion, he offered the natural reasons that occurred to him. Though the pilgrim

---

and was alone on his journey, he began taking the discipline, but he saw this more as a sign of his love for God than as satisfaction for his sins. As for the need to grow in virtue, of this Ignatius was still ignorant, and his mention of discretion perhaps indicates that he thought his former penances should have been regulated by it.

15–16. On leaving Navarrete, Ignatius, who now refers to himself simply as "the pilgrim", went to Logroño and there met the royal highway leading to Saragossa, the capital of Aragón. He passed through Calahorra and Tudela, and as he was approaching Pedrola, a town some twenty-three miles west of Saragossa, he had his strange encounter with a Moor. They fell into conversation, and since their discussion focused on our Lady, it is not difficult to surmise that Ignatius must have told him that he was on his way to Montserrat to visit our Lady's shrine. Because Muslims are faithful readers of the Koran, they hold Mary, the mother of Jesus, in esteem. Together with Christians they maintain that our Lord was miraculously conceived in Mary's womb, for the Koran states: "She said: 'O my Lord! How shall I have a son when no man has touched me?'" [7] But they separate from Christians when they teach that Jesus' birth was natural. On this point the Koran reads: "So she conceived him, and she retired with him to a remote place. And the pains of childbirth drove her to the trunk of a palm tree and she cried in anguish." [8]

---

[7] Sūra 3:47.
[8] Sūra 19:22–23.

countered with many arguments, he could not alter the Moor's opinion. The Moor then went on ahead in great haste so that he lost sight of him. Being left behind, he reflected on what had taken place between himself and the Moor. Various emotions welled up in him, and he became disturbed in soul, thinking that he had failed to do what he should have done. Filled with anger against the Moor and thinking that he had done wrong in allowing a Moor to utter such things about our Lady, he concluded that he was obliged to restore her honor. He now desired to search out the Moor and strike him with his dagger for all that he had said. This conflict in his desires remained with him for some time, but in the end he was still uncertain, for he did not know what was required of him. The Moor, who had gone on ahead, had told him that he was going to a place a little farther on the same route, near the royal highway, but that the highway did not pass through the place.

16. Tired of trying to figure out what would be the good thing to do, and unable to come to any definite decision, he determined on the following, namely, to give the mule free rein and to let it go by itself to the point where the roads met. If the mule took the road to the village, he would then

Hearing the Moor's position on our Lady's perpetual virginity, Ignatius brought forward as many arguments as he could to prove that Mary was not only a virgin before Jesus' birth, but also during and after it. Feeling that the discussion was becoming somewhat heated and seeing that Ignatius had a sword at his side, the Moor abruptly spurred his donkey onward and left Ignatius far behind. The code of chivalry, with which Ignatius was brought up and according to whose tenets he had lived his life, told him that he had done grievous wrong in permitting an infidel to insult our Lady. Thus the Amadís in Ignatius urged him to use his dagger on the Moor, but the Ignatius who fell in love with the saints knew that those who took up the sword would die by the sword. Thus, he was torn by an search out the Moor and use his dagger on him; if the mule took the highway and not the village road, he would then let the Moor go. And he did just as he decided. Our Lord brought it about that though the village was little more than thirty or forty paces away and the road leading to it was quite wide and in good condition, the mule chose the highway and disregarded the village road.

Coming to a large town before reaching Montserrat, he there wanted to purchase the clothes he intended to wear when he went to Jerusalem. He bought some sackcloth—it was of a loose weave and bristly to the touch—and asked

---

internal conflict. Unable to decide what to do, he determined to leave the matter in God's hands. As his mule was coming to a fork in the road that led to Pedrola,[9] where the Moor had gone, he placed the reins in his lap and waited to see which road the mule would take. Would it continue on the highway, or would it go down to Pedrola? Since the mule chose to remain on the highway, Ignatius interpreted this as God's will.

After meeting with the Moor, Ignatius passed through Saragossa— without stopping, for he deliberately avoided crowds—and after traversing some 150 more miles he came to Igualada, a town situated at the foot of Montserrat. Before ascending the craggy mountain, he thought it time to purchase the few items he would need for his journey to Jerusalem. Igualada[10] was known for cloth-making, and there Ignatius bought some rough burlap-type cloth that the local people used for making sacks, and he had a long tunic made for himself. In addition he purchased a gourd for water, and a staff to aid his walking. This was to be his new wardrobe, the wardrobe of the saints. Once he had placed the smaller items in

---

[9] *IdL* 138 states that it was to Pedrola that the Moor had gone. The geographical details provided by Ignatius well describe the approach to Pedrola; the royal highway does not pass through it, but there is a road branching from the highway leading to it.

[10] Earlier authors have been of the opinion that the place where Ignatius made his purchases was Lérida; modern authors think it was Igualada. Lérida is a city, while Igualada is a large town and was known for its cloth. Besides, it was but a short distance from Montserrat. See *IdL* 141 and *IL* 53–54.

them to make it into a long garment that would go down to
his feet. He bought himself a pilgrim's staff and a small hol-
low gourd and attached everything to the saddle atop his
mule.

17. He continued his way to Montserrat thinking, as he
usually did, of the achievements he was going to perform for
the love of God. Because his thoughts were fully occupied
with exploits, such as he had read in *Amadís de Gaula* and
other like books, similar thoughts also came to mind. He
therefore determined to keep a night's vigil over his arms; he

his saddlebag, he turned his mule toward the road that pilgrims used to
reach the shrine on top of the "serrated mountain". After some twenty
days of travel, and having covered some 350 miles,[11] Ignatius was now
ready to present himself before our Lady.

17. It was March 21, 1522, when Ignatius climbed the road to the shrine.
As the mule ascended the mountain slope, so did Ignatius' thoughts as-
cend on high, for he was now filled with thoughts of what he was about
to do. The feast of the Annunciation was approaching; he would make his
confession, divest himself of his rich robes and invest himself in pilgrim's
garb, and then make his vigil before our Lady's statue. From his reading of
the fourth book of *Amadís de Gaula,* Ignatius recalled how Amadís' son,
Esplandián, on the occasion of his consecration as a knight, made his vigil
of arms before a statue of the Blessed Virgin. Ignatius was determined to
do the same.

Arrived at the shrine, Ignatius stabled his mule, registered at the pilgrims' hostel, and went to pray before our Lady's image. The abbey was
celebrated throughout Europe for its reform movement, but it was because of the dark brown, almost black, statue, which the faithful considered miraculous, that countless pilgrims came to pray in the shrine church.
On his first day Ignatius met the priest assigned to hear the confessions of
the pilgrims, Dom Jean Chanon, a Frenchman, who had come to the
abbey in 1512. Ignatius made known his desire to make a general confession of his life, and to help prepare for it Dom Jean supplied him with a

---

[11] *PY* 75 n. 1 tallies the miles from Loyola to Igualada.

would neither sit nor lie down, but would stand and kneel before the altar of Our Lady of Montserrat, where he had decided to set aside the garments he was wearing and clothe himself in the livery of Christ. Having left that place, he continued as usual thinking of his projected plans, and when he arrived at Montserrat, he offered a prayer and arranged for a confessor. He made a general confession in writing, which lasted three days, and arranged with his confessor to

manual of prayers and pious exercises.[12] For the next three days Ignatius fasted on bread and water as he followed the meditations in the manual, examined his conscience, and wrote down his life's sins as best he remembered them. Then, on the eve of the Annunciation, he read the list to his confessor and received absolution.

Though Ignatius had been thinking of making a pilgrimage to Jerusalem for some seven months, he had never revealed these plans to anyone. At Montserrat he told them to Dom Jean. He narrated how God had been working in his soul, how he desired to renounce the world and go to Jerusalem and spend his life doing penance for the love of God. Before he took leave of his confessor, Ignatius told him that he was leaving his

---

[12] Until recent years it has been taken for granted that the manual given to Ignatius at Montserrat was the *Ejercitatorio de la vida espiritual*, composed by Abbot García Jiménez de Cisneros and printed at Montserrat in 1500 (see *IdL* 149–50 and *PY* 80–81). A volume entitled *Compendio breve* has been discovered with the subtitle A Brief Resumé of Spiritual Exercises Taken from the Book entitled The Exercise of the Spiritual Life by the Rev. Fr. Fray García de Cisneros. Aimé Solignac, S.J., who has studied the volume (printed in Barcelona in 1555), notes that the work is not a mere resumé of the *Ejercitatorio*, but that the unknown editor, while using much of the original, at the same time added new considerations and used formulas and expressions that are nearer to Ignatius' *Spiritual Exercises* than to the *Ejercitatorio*. Solignac concludes that perhaps Dom Jean gave Ignatius a copy of the *Compendio breve* (if not yet printed, then in manuscript) and that this is what Ignatius used in preparing for his general confession. See A. Solignac, "Le *Compendio breve* de l'*Exercitatorio* de Cisneros et les *Exercices Spirituels*", *Archivum Historicum Societatis Iesu* 63 (1994): 142–59, or his "Le Manuel de Montserrat et les *Exercices* de Saint Ignace", *Christus* 42 (1995): 358–69.

leave his mule behind and to hang his sword and dagger at
our Lady's altar in the church. The confessor was the first
man to whom he revealed his plans, for up to now he had
never told them to any confessor.

18. On the eve of our Lady's feast in March, in the year
1522, he went at night, as secretly as he could, to a poor
man, and, removing all his clothing, he gave it to the poor
man and dressed himself in the garment he so desired to
wear and went to kneel before our Lady's altar. He spent the
entire night there, sometimes on his knees, sometimes standing erect, with his pilgrim's staff in hand. At break of day he
departed so as not to be recognized, and he took, not the
main road that led directly to Barcelona, on which road he
could meet many who knew and respected him, but a de-

---

mule[13] to the monastery and asked that his dagger and sword be placed
with the other ex-votos on the walls or grille of our Lady's chapel.

18. As evening came on, March 24, the last things Ignatius had to give
away were the very clothes he was wearing, and, finding a beggar at the
shrine, he gave him his robes and donned his pilgrim's tunic. With only a
staff in hand, he went to the church and chose a place before the grille
that separated our Lady's chapel from the body of the church. Other pilgrims were also there preparing themselves for our Lady's great feast. Ignatius stood among them unnoticed, an ordinary pilgrim among others,
offering prayers to our Lady. Ignatius watched in our Lady's presence,
asking her to take him under her protection. This vigil was Ignatius' public consecration as a knight of the Eternal King. He had already offered
himself to his King at Loyola, but that was a private dedication. At this
shrine, with other pilgrims as witnesses, he reconsecrated himself to God
and to His enterprise. That night he entered a new service; he now had a
new Lord.

As day was about to break, monks filed into the chapel and began singing anthems in honor of the Virgin. Ignatius then participated in the Mass

---

[13] The mule was still at the monastery in 1541 when Fr. Antonio Araoz,
Ignatius' nephew, visited there (*FN* 2:522 n. 27).

tour to a town called Manresa, where he decided he would remain for several days in a hospital and jot down a few items in the book that he guardedly carried with him and that afforded him much consolation.

After he had traveled about a league from Montserrat, a man who had been pursuing him caught up with him and asked if he had given some clothing to a certain poor man as the poor man claimed. As he answered that he had done so, tears of compassion rolled from his eyes on behalf of the man to whom he had given his clothes—tears of compassion because he realized that the man was now being suspected of having stolen them. For as much as he fled the esteem of others, he was not long in Manresa before people were saying great things about him, all because of what had happened at Montserrat. His reputation grew, and the people were saying more than what was true: that he had renounced a huge inheritance and other such things.

that followed and received Holy Communion. When the Mass was over he immediately left to be on his way. His hasty departure from the shrine can be accounted for by his desire not to be recognized as the noble who had come in robes but was now leaving in sackcloth.

He limped his way down the mountain with his soul filled with consolation and his mind teeming with thoughts. He needed time to ponder them, to relish them more fully. Rather than going directly to Barcelona to get passage for Italy and the Holy Land, he looked for some out-of-the-way place where he could spend a few days continuing his reflections and have the time to write down in his book the thoughts that had come to him while at Montserrat. Thus, not knowing what was before him, he avoided the royal highway and took a side road that would eventually lead him to Manresa.

Chapter 3

Manresa: Taught by God

(March 25, 1522–Mid-March 1523)

19. While in Manresa he begged alms every day. He ate no meat, nor did he drink wine, though both were offered him. On Sundays he did not fast, and if someone gave him wine, he drank it. And because he had been quite meticulous in caring for his hair, which was according to the fashion of the day—and he had a good crop of hair—he decided to let it grow naturally without combing, cutting, or covering it with anything either during the day or night. For the same reason he let the nails of his feet and hands grow, since he had also been overly neat with regard to them. While

19. During the morning of March 25, 1522, as Ignatius slowly made his way down the mountain, he met four ladies (Inés Pascual, Paula Amigant, Catalina Molins, and Jerónima Claver), all returning home after having visited the shrine.[1] He asked them whether they knew of a hospital nearby, where he could stay and recollect himself for a few days. All four were from Manresa, and since the last named happened to be a nurse at the Hospital of Saint Lucy, it was there that they directed him. They entered Manresa, crossing over the old Roman bridge spanning the Cardoner River,

---

[1] We know of this meeting and the ladies' names from the testimony of Juan Pascual, son of one of them, given during the process leading to Ignatius' beatification. *GV* 205–6.

living in this hospital it many times happened that in full daylight he saw a form in the air near him, and this form gave him much consolation because it was exceedingly beautiful. He did not understand what it really was, but it

and Ignatius headed for the hospital, located, as usual in those times, outside the town's walls.[2] The hospital was for the sick poor and had been in operation since the thirteenth century. In exchange for a bed the pilgrim helped about the hospital, and his food he begged in the city. He originally planned to spend but a few days there and then go on to Barcelona so that he could be in Italy by late spring to meet the pilgrim ship going to Jerusalem. But the few days turned into ten months. Ignatius does not tell us what changed his mind. Was it the plague in Barcelona during the spring of 1522 that prevented him from going there, or did he feel that he must better prepare himself by greater penance? Whatever the reason, he remained in Manresa and imitated the eccentric Egyptian hermit Saint Onuphrius, or Humphrey, who, as he had read in the *Golden Legend*, let his hair grow until his entire body was covered. Intent on gaining a complete mastery over himself, Ignatius too let his hair grow long and wild and no longer cared for the nails on his hands and feet.[3]

Ignatius' early days in Manresa were days of peace and spiritual joy. He found a cave where he went to pray and to do penance. He was accustomed to spending seven hours a day in prayer, taking the discipline three times a day, working in the hospital, begging his daily food, and attending services in the local church. It was at Manresa that he saw—and not once

---

[2] Next to the hospital was a chapel dedicated to Saint Lucy, and the tradition in Manresa is that in mid-December 1522, Ignatius there experienced a rapture that lasted eight days. The hospital was converted into an inn in 1575, and in 1601 the property came into the possession of the Society, which then converted the building into a residence and later (1622) built a college next door. These buildings were destroyed during Spain's civil war during the first half of the twentieth century. A new church from 1948 stands there today and bears the name "El Rapte". See I. Puig, *Recuerdos Ignacianas en Manresa* (Barcelona, 1949).

[3] See Pedro Leturia, "El influjo de San Onofre en San Ignacio a base de un texto de Nadal", in *Estudios Ignacianos* (Rome: Institutum Historicum S. I., 1957), 1:97–111.

somehow seemed to have the shape of a serpent and had many things that shone like eyes, but were not eyes. He received much delight and consolation from gazing upon this object, and the more he looked upon it, the more his consolation increased, but when the object vanished he became disconsolate.

20. Up to this time he continued undisturbed in the same interior state of great and constant joy without knowing anything about internal spiritual matters. During the days that the vision lasted, or a little before it began—for it endured many days—a disturbing thought came to torment him, pointing out to him the burdensomeness of his life. It was like someone speaking within his soul: "And how will you be able to put up with this for the seventy years you have ahead of you?" Perceiving that this was the voice of the enemy, he likewise interiorly answered and with great courage: "Oh, you wretch! Can you promise me one hour of life?" Thus he

or twice but sometimes several times a day—that strange serpentine form with its seven or eight shining eyes that were not really eyes.[4] Ignatius at first did not know what this form was or what it meant, but sometime later, as he explains in no. 31, he came to know that it was the devil, and though he then recognized it for what it was, nevertheless, that form continued to appear for the next fifteen years, that is, until Ignatius arrived in Rome.

20. During his days of consolation Ignatius was faced with this temptation: the manner of life that he had chosen was impossible to live; he could do it for a time, but never persevere until death. Since he had already made his decision to follow Christ, and now having refused to go back on his word, the temptation vanished. He notes that the temptation occurred at the time he was entering the church where he usually went to attend Mass and participate in the Divine Office. This church was prob-

---

[4] Polanco gives these details in his *Summarium*, no. 17. See *FN* 1:160.

overcame the temptation and remained tranquil. This was the first temptation he experienced after the above incident, and it happened as he was going to the church where he daily attended High Mass as well as Vespers and Compline, which were always sung, and from which he derived great consolation. He usually read the Passion at Mass, always maintaining his soul in peaceful serenity.

21. After the above-mentioned temptation, he began to feel notable changes in his soul. Sometimes he was so dejected that he found no enjoyment in the prayers he recited, not even in attending Mass, or in any other form of prayer. Sometimes the exact opposite happened to him, and so suddenly that it seemed he had stripped away all sadness and desolation, just as one strips a cloak from one's shoulders.

ably the collegiate church called the Seo,[5] since Manresa had once been an episcopal see. With him he had a *Book of Hours*, a prayer book containing the psalms and prayers for the different parts of the Divine Office. During Ignatius' time these books usually included the Passion narrative from Saint John's Gospel or a harmonized version of the Passion based on the four evangelists.[6]

21. Ignatius now enters the second stage of his spiritual development, a period of darkness of soul. His attendance at Mass sometimes produced consolation, but at other times it brought about arid desolation. Because he was still a beginner in the way of the spiritual life, he was unable to interpret what was happening to him, but he recognized that something profound was taking place in his soul, and this made him wonder: "What

---

[5] The church, known in Manresa as the Basilica de la Seu, was begun in 1328, and when Ignatius frequented it, it was not yet completed. The gothic structure stands on high ground overlooking the city, and it is the first building that the visitor approaching Manresa from the Cardoner sees.

[6] Father Balduin Delange recalled, in 1598, that Ignatius had once told him, in 1551, that he had used such a book at the time of his conversion (*FN* 1:392 n. 5).

He was astonished at these changes, which he had never before experienced, and said to himself: "What kind of a new life is this that we are now beginning?" At this time he sometimes spoke with spiritual persons who respected him and desired to converse with him, and though he had no knowledge of spiritual matters, nevertheless, his words manifested a great fervor and a firm will to advance in God's service.

There was in Manresa, at the time, a woman advanced in years, who had been for a long time a servant of God and was known as such in many parts of Spain, so much so that the Catholic King had once summoned her to seek her advice. One day this woman, chatting with Christ's new soldier, said to him: "May it please my Lord Jesus Christ to appear to you some day!" He was quite surprised at her remark and, understanding the words in a literal way, asked: "How would Jesus Christ appear to me?" Every Sunday he continued his usual custom of confessing his sins and receiving Communion.

kind of a new life is this that we are now beginning?" Considered by some in Manresa to be a spiritual person—though Ignatius claimed that he had no knowledge of spiritual matters—individuals sought his advice, seeking to learn how they could better serve God. He does not tell us who these individuals were, but among those with whom he spoke, one especially impressed him, and that was an elderly woman who was sufficiently famous for King Ferdinand to request to see her. This woman still remains unknown despite the efforts of Ignatius' biographers to identify her. Then, almost as an afterthought, he mentions his custom of going to confession and of receiving Holy Communion each week. This custom had probably been recommended to him by his confessor Dom Jean Chanon at Montserrat, and he, in turn, recommended it to all who sought his advice. Weekly Communion was uncommon in the sixteenth century, and the Church had to wait until the time of Pope Saint Pius X, in the early part of the twentieth century, to change her custom.

22. Now he began to be greatly troubled with scruples. Though he had made a general confession at Montserrat and had done so with great care, having written everything out, as it was said, at times it still seemed to him that he had not confessed certain things. This brought him much suffering, for even though he had confessed everything he was still not satisfied. Thus he began to look about for some spiritual men who would cure him of his scruples, but nothing helped him. Finally, a learned man connected with the cathedral chapter, who was a very spiritual man and who used to preach there, one day told him in confession to write down all that he could remember. This he did, but even after he had confessed all this, his scruples returned even with regard to small and piddling matters, so that he was deeply distressed. Though he understood that these scruples were doing him much harm and it would be good to be free of them, still he could not cast them off. He sometimes thought that his cure would lie in his confessor ordering him in the name of Jesus Christ not to confess anything more from his past life, and he desired his confessor so to order him, but he did not dare suggest this to him.

23. Without having to ask, his confessor did order him not to confess anything more from his past unless it was something abundantly clear. But since he considered everything manifestly clear, the order benefitted him not at all, and thus he continued in his anxiety. At this time he was living in a

22–24. Some time after his arrival in Manresa, Ignatius was severely tormented by scruples. He felt that he had not confessed certain of his sins as he should have, and though he confessed them again and again his soul was without peace. He sought help from various priests, but none was able to help him. He notes that he went to confession to the priest who

small room that the Dominicans had given him in their monastery, and there he kept his custom of praying seven hours a
day on his knees, of rising every midnight, and of performing all the other exercises previously mentioned. In all this
he found no cure for his scruples; they had now been tor-
menting him for several months. Once, being very disturbed
because of them, he set himself to pray, and with great fervor
he cried aloud to God, saying: "Help me, Lord, for I find no
remedy among men, nor in any creature. No task would be
too irksome for me if I thought I could get help. Lord, show
me where I may get it, and even if I have to follow after a
little puppy to get the remedy I need, I will do it."

24. Taken up with these thoughts he was many times ve-
hemently tempted to throw himself into a deep hole in his
room, which was near the place where he used to pray. But
realizing that it was a sin to kill oneself, he again cried out:
"Lord, I will do nothing to offend You." He many times

---

regularly preached at the cathedral,[7] and following his advice he made
another general confession as he had done at Montserrat, but still without
peace. By this time he had left his room at the Saint Lucy Hospital and
was living in a cell on the ground floor of the Dominican monastery,[8]
which the monks had kindly offered him. He took his problem to his
Dominican confessor,[9] but his burden never left him. Ignatius, nevertheless, continued his prayers and penance, and at midnight rose to attend
Matins in the Dominican church. Having suffered his scruples for several
months, Ignatius was prepared to try any remedy, no matter how difficult

---

[7] The name of the priest assigned to preach at the Seo in 1552 was Juan
Boutabi. See *IL* 60.

[8] This monastery's church was dedicated to Saint Peter Martyr. Tradition in
Manresa has it that Ignatius transferred to this monastery from the hospital on
April 1. The Dominican church was destroyed in 1835, but the plaza there still
bears the name of Saint Dominic.

[9] Tradition identifies him as Guillermo de Pellarós, O.P. See *FN* 1:394 n. 10.

repeated these words as well as the former ones. He remembered the story of a saint who, in order to obtain from God something he very much desired, went without eating for many days until he received it. Spending much time thinking of this idea, he finally decided to do the same, telling himself that he would neither eat nor drink until God had granted his request, or until he saw that death was near. For if he saw himself *in extremis* and was about to die because of not eating, he decided that he would then ask for bread and eat it (for in such extreme circumstances he would be permitted to ask for it and eat it).

or how ridiculous, if only he could find relief. So debilitating was this torment that he even contemplated suicide,[10] but then he remembered what Saint Andrew, whom he encountered in his reading, had once done. In imitation of him Ignatius decided neither to eat nor to drink anything until God had freed him of his scruples.[11]

---

[10] The text clearly states that there was a deep hole (*agujero*) in the room, but it is difficult to imagine a deep hole in the very room where Ignatius was living. Some authors have thus interpreted *agujero* to be a large opening or window through which Ignatius was tempted to throw himself (see *IL* 62). Since Ignatius' room, according to tradition among the Dominicans, was on ground level, it is difficult to conceive how jumping from a window but a few feet from the ground would be attempting suicide! Hence, there are those who postulate that next to Ignatius' room were deep excavations, and that he was tempted to jump through the window into the excavations (see *St. Ignatius' Own Story*, trans. William J. Young, S.J. [Chicago: Regnery, 1956], 20). Since the Dominican monastery, where Ignatius had once resided, was destroyed in 1860, there is no way of solving this difficulty.

[11] *FN* 1:397 n. 12 suggests that this was the apostle Saint Andrew, for according to the *Golden Legend*, he is supposed to have said that he would not eat until God had granted pardon to a certain Nicholas. Andrew then fasted for five days, after which period an angel came to him and notified him that Nicholas had been pardoned through the apostle's prayers. See Jacobus de Voragine, *The Golden Legend: Readings on the Saints*, trans. William Granger Ryan (Princeton: Princeton University, 1993), 1:14–15.

25. One Sunday, after he had received Communion, he started his fast. He went through an entire week without putting anything in his mouth, but at the same time he continued his usual exercises, participating in the Divine Office, praying on his knees, rising at midnight, and so forth. When the following Sunday came, it was again time for him to go to confession, and since he was in the habit of telling his confessor everything he did with all its details, he also told him how he had eaten nothing that week. The confessor ordered him to break off his fast, and though he was still feeling strong, he nevertheless obeyed his confessor, and that day as well as the following day he found that he was free of his scruples. But on the third day, which was Tuesday, the remembrance of his sins returned to him while he was at prayer, and as one thing leads to another, he thought of sin after sin from his past life and felt obliged to confess them again. After these thoughts, there came upon him a loathing for the life he was then living, and he had a strong temptation to give it up. In this manner the Lord chose to awaken him as from a dream. Now that he had some experience with the different spirits—through the lessons that God had given him—he began to think about the way that that spirit had come to him. Thus he decided, and with great clarity of mind, never to confess his past sins again, and from that day forward he was free of his scruples, and he held it for certain

25. By obeying his confessor with regard to giving up his fast, Ignatius' scruples left for a time, but they returned, and with them the temptation to abandon his new way of life. It was this temptation that awakened him, as if from a deep sleep, for he now understood whence those scruples had come, and his decision never again to confess his past sins brought him the freedom he had sought for so long a time. Ignatius does not attribute this freedom to anything that he himself may have done, but views it as a gift of God's mercy.

that our Lord had desired to set him free because of His mercy.

26. In addition to his seven hours of prayer, he spent time in helping other souls who came there to see him about spiritual matters, and the rest of the day he gave to thinking about the things of God that he had read or meditated on that day. But often when he went to bed, great spiritual lights came to him, as did wonderful consolations, so that they took up most of the time that he had set aside for sleep, which was not much. Now and then reflecting on this loss of sleep, he considered how he had allotted a fixed amount of time each day to converse with God, and then the remainder of the day as well, and thus he came to doubt whether those lights came from the good spirit. He concluded that it was better to set them aside and sleep the allotted time. This he did.

26. Among the books Ignatius had at Manresa and which he used for his meditations was *The Imitation of Christ*, attributed today to Thomas à Kempis, but in Ignatius' time also to Jean Gerson, the one-time Chancellor of the University of Paris. Ignatius affectionately called it his "Little Gerson". Later in life he affirmed: "It was at Manresa that I saw the *Gerçonzito* for the first time, and since then there is no other book of devotion that I like more."[12] Though Ignatius was no longer plagued by scruples, he was not totally free of the devil's subtle activity, for when it was time to sleep, his mind filled with spiritual lights so that he was losing the sleep he sorely needed. Knowing well that he had not disregarded God during the day, but had given Him many hours in prayer and reflection, Ignatius concluded that these lights were but another manifestation of the devil's wiles, and thus he cast them aside and slept the few hours he had allotted himself.

---

[12] *FN* 1:584; in the same place Gonçalves da Câmara also records that Ignatius read a chapter of *The Imitation* each day of his life. For a more detailed treatment of Ignatius' use of *The Imitation*, see J. N. Tylenda, "The Books that Led Ignatius to God", *Review for Religious* 57 (1998): 286–98.

27. He continued in his resolve to abstain from eating meat and was so firm in that decision that for nothing would he think of changing it. Then one morning, after he got out of bed, some meat appeared before him just as if he saw it with his body's eyes, though he had had no prior craving for it. At the same time a powerful inclination of will came over him henceforth to eat meat. Though he remembered his earlier resolve, still he did not hesitate to decide that he ought to eat meat. Later on, when he related this to his confessor, the confessor told him to study the matter to see, if by chance, it was a temptation. After putting it through a thorough examination he was sure that it was not.

During this period God was dealing with him in the same way a schoolteacher deals with a child while instructing him. This was either because he was thick and dull of brain or because of the firm will that God Himself had implanted in him to serve Him—but he clearly recognized and has always recognized that it was in this way that God dealt with him. Furthermore, if he were to doubt this, he would think he was offending the Divine Majesty. One can see how God dealt with him in the following five examples.

27. During his months in Manresa, Ignatius sought spiritual guidance from many individuals but found none able to offer him what he needed. Having gone through months of darkness of soul, he finally learned that his teacher in all this was our Lord Himself. Ignatius was but a child in the school of the spiritual life, and it was our Lord who taught him how to discern the spirits that were moving him and enabled him to see that both abstaining from meat and eating of the same may be equally praiseworthy. In Christian tradition Ignatius is known for his development of the art of the discernment of spirits. As a result of the diversity of spirits that he experienced at Loyola and at Manresa, he learned how to distinguish them and came to know what was God's will for him. The knowledge that Ignatius gained from these experiences may be found in the "Rules for the Discernment of Spirits" in his *Spiritual Exercises.*

28. First. He was greatly devoted to the Most Holy Trinity, and every day he prayed to each of the three Persons. But while doing the same to the Most Holy Trinity, the thought came to him, why four prayers to the Trinity? But this thought caused him little or no trouble since it was of so little importance. One day, as he was saying the Hours of Our Lady on the monastery's steps, his understanding was raised on high, so as to see the Most Holy Trinity under the aspect of three keys on a musical instrument, and as a result he shed many tears and sobbed so strongly that he could not control himself. Joining in a procession that came out of the monastery, that morning he could not hold back his tears until

28. Of the many things that Ignatius learned under our Lord's guidance, he calls attention to five special graces, five privileged moments when the divine intruded into his life and touched him most intimately. It was now time for his soul to pass from darkness into the light of mystical grace. Ignatius offers no lengthy explanations of these graces. Rather, he chooses to remain relatively silent about them. If these are not listed in chronological order of their occurrence, then he begins with the most fundamental.

The prayer books of the sixteenth century usually contained prayers to each of the three Persons of the Trinity, together with an added fourth prayer to the Triune God. Ignatius wondered about the need for this fourth prayer, but he also recognized that his question was of little moment. His reflections on the Trinity were soon to be resolved by an extraordinary grace. One morning, as he was about to enter the Dominican church with his thoughts focused on the Trinity, he was given to understand how the three distinct Persons in the Godhead could form a single unity. He saw the three Persons, he says, as three keys on an instrument. Each key having its own individual sound, but when played together, each key, without losing any of its own distinctiveness, contributes itself and together they form a unified harmonic chord. Thus he perceived the distinction of the three Persons, while experiencing the unity of the Godhead. So powerful and overwhelming was this experience that it stayed with him throughout that day. He could do nothing else but think of the Trinity, and when he spoke he had to speak of the Trinity. This was not a transitory grace, dinnertime, and after he had eaten he could not refrain from talking, with much joy and consolation, about the Most Holy Trinity, making use of different comparisons. This experience remained with him for the rest of his life, so that whenever he prayed to the Most Holy Trinity he felt great devotion.

29. Second. One day it was granted him to understand, with great spiritual joy, the way in which God had created the world. He seemed to see a white object with rays stemming from it, from which God made light. He neither knew how to explain these things nor did he fully remember the spiritual lights that God had then imprinted on his soul.

for it remained with him for the rest of his life, as his *Spiritual Journal*[13] amply attests.[14]

29. Another exceptional mystical grace was to behold how everything in creation proceeded from the Triune God as rays stemming from a white object. This vision is closely connected with the previous one, because creation is the proper external activity of the Trinity. Ignatius offers no further elucidation and perhaps nor should we. He, in fact, says, that he did not know how to explain what he had seen. At least we can say this: as rays burst forth from light and carry light with them, so creation comes forth from God and manifests God in it. The emphasis here is not on the created object, that is, the created world outside God, but on the burning source of that creation. God is all love, and as such, He has to show His love, and, thus, it bursts forth into creation.

The third privileged moment at Manresa deals with Christ in the Eucharist. At the moment of the elevation of the host during Mass at the Dominican church, Ignatius inwardly saw white rays coming from above and clearly understood how our Lord is present in that Sacrament. As for any explanation, he could never offer one that would prove adequate.

---

[13] See *Spiritual Journal of Ignatius Loyola, February 2, 1544 to February 27, 1545,* trans. William J. Young, S.J. (Woodstock, Md.: Woodstock College, 1958).

[14] Diego Laínez, in a 1547 letter, states that Ignatius' thoughts were so taken up with the Trinity that he had thought of and had actually begun writing a book on the subject. Evidently nothing ever came of it (*FN* 1:82).

Third. It was likewise in Manresa—where he stayed for almost a year, and after experiencing divine consolations and seeing the fruit that he was bringing forth in the souls he was helping—that he abandoned those extremes he had previously practiced and began to cut his nails and hair. One day, while in town and attending Mass in the church attached to the above-mentioned monastery, he saw with inward eyes, at the time of the elevation of the Body of the Lord, some white ray coming from above. But after so long a time he is now unable adequately to explain this; nevertheless, he clearly saw with his understanding how our Lord Jesus Christ was present in that Most Holy Sacrament.

Fourth. During prayer he often, and for an extended period of time, saw with inward eyes the humanity of Christ, whose form appeared to him as a white body, neither very large nor very small; nor did he see any differentiation of members. He often saw this in Manresa; and if he were to say twenty times for forty times, he would not presume to say that he was lying. He saw it again when he was in Jerusalem, and once more when he was on his way to Padua. He has also seen our Lady in similar form, without differentiation of members. These things that he saw at that time fortified him and gave such great support to his faith that many times he thought to himself: If there were no Scriptures to

The fourth deals with our Lord's humanity. Again with inward eyes, Ignatius saw Christ's humanity as well as that of our Lady, but without differentiation of members. He goes on to note that this vision of Christ was of rather frequent occurrence, and not only in Manresa but also when he was traveling to Padua (see no. 41) and while in the Holy Land (see no. 48). So vivid and so powerful were these interior illuminations that he said he could not doubt their truthfulness and that he would willingly give his life for them.

teach us these matters of faith, he would still resolve to die for them on the basis of what he had seen.

30. Fifth. He was once on his way, out of devotion, to a church a little more than a mile from Manresa, which I think was called Saint Paul. The road followed the path of the river, and he was taken up with his devotions; he sat down for a while facing the river flowing far below him. As he sat there

All these graces came to him at the time that he was sought after as a spiritual guide. Seeing that his contacts with other spiritual-minded persons were bearing fruit, and fearing that his appearance might keep some from visiting him and thereby deprive them of the help he could offer them, Ignatius abandoned the extreme measures he had adopted from Saint Onuphrius and once again cut his hair and nails.

30–31. The fifth grace, and the most important, was the decisive moment in Ignatius' spiritual development. One day,[15] as he was walking toward the church of Saint Paul the Hermit, the church attached to the nearby Cistercian monastery,[16] Ignatius was so caught up in his thoughts that he sat down overlooking the Cardoner and continued his reflections. God flooded his soul with extraordinary light, giving him a profound insight into and a feeling for the mysteries of the faith. He now understood these truths with such a clarity that even though he had reflected on them in the past they were as totally new to him. He now perceived everything in its proper relationship to God. These truths, furthermore, were so encompassing that what he had learned on that one occasion was more than he had learned since that event. Together with the broader under-

---

[15] Polanco says (*FN* 1:160) that this vision took place four months after Ignatius' conversion, but since he does not date the time of that conversion, there is no way of knowing when this illumination occurred. The chronology in *OC* 41 suggests that it may have been in August or September 1522.

[16] The monastery and church of Saint Paul the Hermit were situated on the banks of the Cardoner and had been under the care of the Cistercians since 1472. In 1699 the monastery was sold to the Jesuits, who then rebuilt the house and restored the chapel. In 1767 the Society lost the property by Charles III's decree expelling the Jesuits from his realm. At that time the house went into private hands. See *OC* 108 n. 4.

the eyes of his understanding were opened, and though he saw no vision, he understood and perceived many things, numerous spiritual things as well as matters touching on faith and learning, and this was with an elucidation so bright that all these things seemed new to him. He cannot expound in detail what he then understood, for there were many things, but he can state that he received such a lucidity in understanding that during the course of his entire life—now having passed his sixty-second year—if he were to gather all the helps he received from God and everything he knew, and add them together, he does not think they would add up to all that he received on that one occasion.

31. After this lasted for some time, he went to kneel before a cross, which was near that place, to give thanks to God, and there that vision appeared to him—the one that had appeared many times before and which he had never understood—that is, the object described earlier that seemed most beautiful to him, with its many eyes. Kneeling before the cross he noticed that the object was without the beautiful color it usually had, and he distinctly understood, and felt the firm agreement of his will, that that was the evil spirit. Many times later it continued to appear to him, but as a mark of his disdain for it he drove it away with the pilgrim's staff he always had in his hand.

standing of the faith Ignatius received a fuller realization of his vocation and possessed a clearer determination to follow Christ. At the illumination's end, Ignatius walked a bit farther to the Cross of Tort, and there he spilled out his gratitude to God for the graces granted him. It was while kneeling before that cross that the vision of the serpentine form (see no. 19) appeared, but in the light of his most recent enlightenment, he immediately detected that the shiny form with eyes that were not eyes was the evil spirit. It was no longer attractive. Whenever it again appeared he would brandish his staff, and it would immediately disappear.

32. On one occasion, while in Manresa, having fallen ill with a high fever and being on the point of death, he was quite certain that his soul was about to depart his body. At that instant the thought came into his mind that he was numbered among the righteous, but this brought him so much distress that he tried everything to dismiss it and to dwell on his sins. He had more difficulty with that than with the fever, but no matter how he toiled to overcome it, he was unable to do so. When the fever lessened and he was no longer in danger of death, he loudly cried out to certain ladies who had come to visit him that the next time they saw him at death's door they were, for the love of God, to shout aloud that he was a sinner and that he should be ever mindful of the sins he had committed against God.

33. On another occasion, when he was traveling from Valencia to Italy by sea, the ship's rudder was smashed in a

---

32. Because of the severe penances that Ignatius had been in the habit of practicing, it is no wonder that he several times fell ill in Manresa. The incident here recorded may have taken place during the summer of 1522. He had been praying at the shrine of Our Lady of Villadordis, about a mile from Manresa, and was found unconscious by a passerby. He was taken to the hospital, and from there the Amigant family took him into its home and cared for him. [17] With his body burning with fever, Ignatius was certain that death was soon to take him, but the thought of death did not cause him fear. When the fever had passed and after he had recognized those caring for him, he asked that if he should ever again become ill they were to remind him that he was nothing but a sinner.

33. The remembrance of his nearness to death in Manresa led Ignatius to think of two other incidents in his life, and in both there was joy and not fear. The first took place in 1535 when he boarded a vessel in Valencia

---

[17] See *GV* 222. Paula Amigant was one of the four ladies Ignatius met coming down from Montserrat. The Amigant house still stands, and next to it is the chapel "Ignacio Enfermo".

violent storm, and being in a crisis, he and many other passengers aboard concluded that, as things then stood, they would
not be able to escape death. Thus making use of his time, he
made a careful examination of conscience and prepared himself for death, but he felt no fear because of his sins nor was he
afraid of being condemned. He was, however, especially disturbed and sorry, knowing that he had not put to good use all
the gifts and graces that God our Lord had granted him.

In the year 1550, he was once more gravely ill, due to a serious sickness that, in his own judgment and that of others, was
to be his last. Thinking of death at the time, he experienced
such joy and so much spiritual consolation in the thought of
having to die that he burst into tears. This came to be of such
frequent occurrence that many times he stopped thinking of
death so as not to have so much consolation.

34. When winter came, he became sick with a severe illness, and in order that he could recover, the city placed him
in the house of the father of a certain Ferrera, who later

to go to Genoa—he was on his way to meet his companions in Venice,
intending to go with them on pilgrimage to the Holy Land. The second
was when Ignatius was in Rome and had been sick from the end of 1550
to the beginning of 1551.[18]

34. Ignatius' final illness in Manresa was during the winter of 1522, and,
because he was so greatly esteemed, the city saw that he had proper care
and placed him in the house of Antonio Benito Ferrer.[19] Ignatius well
remembered that family because Antonio's son later entered the service of
Baltasar da Faria, who had been the King of Portugal's agent in Rome
during the years 1543–1551.[20] The ladies[21] who cared for Ignatius

---

[18] See *FN* 1:408 n. 27.

[19] See *OC* 110 n. 20; Ferrer is the modern form of the name.

[20] See ibid.

[21] *OC* 100 n. 22 identifies these as Inés Pascual, Angela Amigant, Micaela
Canyelles, Inés Clavera, and Brianda Paguera. See *GV* 211 n. 10.

entered the service of Baltasar de Faria. There he was assid-
uously cared for, and many important ladies, who were devoted to him, came to watch through the night. He recovered
from his illness, but he nevertheless remained weak and frequently suffered stomach pains. Because of his condition and
because the winter was most severe, the ladies made him
dress properly, wear shoes, and cover his head. Thus they
made him accept two brown-colored jackets, made of very
coarse cloth, and a beret of the same material as a cap. During this time there were many days when he was most desirous to talk of spiritual matters and to find some individuals
able to do so. But the time that he had set for his departure
for Jerusalem was fast approaching.

35. At the beginning of the year 1523, he departed for
Barcelona in order to set sail, and though some individuals
offered to accompany him, he wanted to go by himself, for

decided that the simple rough tunic he had been wearing was far from
sufficient to keep him warm during the wintry months, and, thus, they
imposed upon him to accept heavier clothing and suggested that if he
dressed properly and covered his head he would reduce the chances of
again becoming ill. Once Ignatius was able to get about and noted that
spring was coming, his thoughts focused on Jerusalem.

35. After having spent ten months in Manresa, Ignatius left the city in
mid-February 1523.[22] Once he arrived in Barcelona he went to the residence of Inés Pascual,[23] whom he had known in Manresa and whose
house was near the harbor. Ignatius' friends knew that he was seeking

---

[22] FN 1:81 n. 16 suggests that Ignatius left Manresa on February 17 or 18.

[23] Ignatius first met the widow Pascual on his way down from his vigil at
Montserrat. She had a house in Manresa as well as one in Barcelona near the
church of Santa María del Mar. She was one of Ignatius' first benefactresses,
and some of his earliest letters were written to her. Ignatius always felt a debt
of gratitude to her, so much so that when the first Jesuits came to Spain, they
were instructed to call upon her. She died on April 9, 1548, having been
attended by Fr. Antonio Araoz, Ignatius' nephew. See LW 173–74.

his desire was to have only God as his refuge. One day, as his friends were pressing him to take a companion, telling him how helpful a companion would be, since he knew neither Italian nor Latin, and commending one, he answered that even if it were the son or brother of the Duke of Cardona he would not travel with him because he wanted to exercise the virtues of charity, of faith, and of hope. By taking a companion he would expect help from him when he was hungry, and if he should fall, he would expect him to help him get up; consequently he would put his trust in the companion and have affection for him, but he wanted to place his trust, love, and hope in God alone. What he thus said came right from his heart. It was with such a disposition that he wanted to set sail, not only by himself, but also without provisions. In arranging for his passage, he convinced the ship's captain to give him free passage, since he had no money, but on condition that he bring with him enough biscuit to last him through the journey. In no other way in the world would they take him on board.

passage to Italy, but they interpreted this to mean that he was merely going to Rome. They tried to persuade him to take a companion, since he knew neither Latin nor Italian, but he wanted his pilgrimage to be an expression of complete trust in God. In mentioning the Duke of Cardona, Ignatius does so not only because the duke belonged to one of the noblest families in Catalonia, but also because he knew the duke's sister, Juana, who was the wife of his former lord, the Duke of Nájera.[24]

---

[24] Ignatius speaks of no companion. However, during the investigation leading to Ignatius' beatification, Juan Pascual, Inés' son, testified that the priest Antonio Pujol, his mother's brother, traveled with Ignatius to Barcelona and there took him to the Pascual home, where he was given a room on the top floor. The priest was returning to Tarragona, where he was a member of Archbishop Pedro Folch de Cardona's staff (see *LW* 174; *IL* 70).

36. When he was arranging for the biscuit, he began to have great scruples. "Is this the hope and faith you have in the God who would not fail you?" And so on. These thoughts were so persistent that they caused him great distress. Finally, not knowing what he should do because he saw good reasons on both sides, he decided to place himself in the hands of his confessor. He thus told him how greatly he desired to seek perfection and what was for the greater glory of God, as well as the reasons that made him hesitate about taking provisions with him. The confessor decided that he should beg for whatever he needed and to take it with him. As he was begging from a lady, she asked him where he intended to go. At first he hesitated to tell her, but finally said that he was going to Italy and Rome, not daring to say any more. Somewhat astonished, she said: "You want to go to Rome? As for those who go there, no one knows how they will return." By this she meant that those who go to Rome return with little spiritual profit. The reason why he did not dare to say that he was going to Jerusalem was his fear of vainglory; this fear so plagued him that he never dared to say from what country he came, or who his family was. Finally, having obtained the biscuit, he got ready to go aboard. Arriving at the ship, he found that he still had five or six *blancas* left of what he had received begging from door to door—for

36–37. The ship's captain was willing to give Ignatius free passage, but he insisted that Ignatius bring his own provisions. Ignatius saw this as being in conflict with his desire to have full dependence upon God, but his confessor solved his problem by telling him that begging the money for his provisions would still manifest trust in God. Ignatius approached a certain lady for alms, and when she asked his destination, she was startled that it should be Rome, for she was convinced that all who visited there returned in a worse moral state than when they departed. This lady is this was his usual way of supporting himself—and he left the coins on a bench that he found near the shore.

37. After having been in Barcelona a little more than twenty days, he went aboard ship. But while still in Barcelona and before boarding ship, he followed his usual custom of searching out spiritual persons in order to talk to them, and even visited those living in hermitages far from the city. But neither in Barcelona nor in Manresa—for the entire time that he was there—was he able to find individuals who were able to help him as much as he desired. Only in Manresa, that woman we have already mentioned, who told him that she had prayed to God that Jesus Christ would appear to him, she alone seemed to him to have made progress in the spiritual life. Thus, after he left Barcelona, he completely lost his eagerness to search out spiritual persons.

sometimes identified as Isabel Roser,[25] who later became one of Ignatius' closest friends and greatest benefactress. With the money he collected he bought his supply of biscuit, and the few remaining *blancas* he had in his pocket—they were coins of the lowest denomination then in use—he left on a bench for any passerby to pick up.

In Barcelona, as in Manresa, Ignatius attempted to single out spiritual individuals, but over the past months the only one whom he considered to have made progress in the spiritual life was the elderly woman mentioned in no. 21. After three weeks in Barcelona Ignatius was ready to sail for Italy.

---

[25] Isabel Roser lived in Barcelona in a house opposite the church of San Yusto y Pastor, and it was in that church that she first saw Ignatius speaking with children. After inviting him into her home and learning that he was to go to Rome, she is supposed to have uttered the remark about Rome. When she heard that Ignatius was to sail on a brigantine, she persuaded him to go on a larger ship that was likewise in the harbor. After the brigantine set sail, it capsized just outside the harbor and sank with all on board. When Ignatius returned from his Holy Land pilgrimage, he would again discuss his plans with her. See *LW* 262–63.

Chapter 4

Jerusalem: Pilgrim in the Holy Land

(Mid–March–September 22, 1523)

38. With a strong wind behind them, they made the trip from Barcelona to Gaeta in five days and five nights, with everyone still fearful because of the severe storm. Everywhere in that region there was fear of the plague, but as soon as he disembarked he started walking toward Rome. From among those who were aboard ship, a mother and her daughter, who was dressed in boy's clothing, joined him, as did another young man. They accompanied him because they too were begging their way. When they arrived at a large farmhouse, they found a big fire and around it many soldiers who offered them something to eat and gave them much wine, persuading them to drink on, as if, it seemed, they wanted to get them drunk. They separated; the mother and daughter went to an upstairs room, while the pilgrim and

---

38. The vessel carrying Ignatius left Barcelona in mid-March 1523, and since Gaeta, Italy, is almost due east of Barcelona, the vessel traveled something of a straight line, passing through the Strait of Bonifacio, which separates Corsica from Sardinia. Because of favorable winds the crossing took less than a week. Ignatius arrived in Gaeta about March 20 to 22; the city is situated approximately seventy-five miles south of Rome and fifty miles north of Naples.

the young man went to a stable. In the middle of the night he heard loud shouts coming from upstairs, and rising to see what the noise was, he found the mother and daughter in tears in the courtyard below, weeping and lamenting because the soldiers had tried to violate them. So strong an emotion took hold of him that he began to shout out: "Do we have to put up with this?" and similar complaints, which he uttered with such effectiveness that everyone was so dumbfounded that no one laid a hand on him. The young man had already fled, so the three of them continued their journey, though it was still night.

39. When they arrived at a nearby city, they found the gates closed, and being unable to enter, all three of them spent that night in a church, dank from the rain and located outside the city. When morning came the city was closed to them, and because they found no alms outside, they went to a castle that was not far away. There the pilgrim became

39. Since the plague was of frequent occurrence in the sixteenth century, and because it brought many deaths with it, Italian cities were especially careful about admitting strangers within their walls without certificates attesting to their good health. Thus, when Ignatius arrived at this city north of Gaeta, he found the city gates closed. The name of that city has not come down to us, but since it was near Gaeta, two cities have been suggested. Some authors think that because the lady in question understood Ignatius, she herself must have been Spanish, and thus they suggest that the lady was Juana of Aragón, wife of Ascanio Colonna, whose seat was in Paliano. On the other hand, it would not be altogether impossible for an educated Italian lady to understand the simple question that Ignatius had proposed to her in Spanish, and hence other authors suggest that the lady was Beatrice Appiani, wife of Vespasiano Colonna, whose seat was in Fondi.[1]

[1] See *FN* 1:414 n. 2; *OC* 113 n. 1; *GV* 240–41.

weak—as much from the trials at sea as from others—and not being able to continue his way, he remained there while the mother and daughter made for Rome. That day many people came out of the city, and learning that the first lady of that region had also come out, he presented himself before her to tell her that his only infirmity was weakness and asked her permission to enter the city to seek medicine. She promptly granted his request. He started begging in the city and collected a good supply of *quattrini*. Feeling his health return after two days, he continued his journey and arrived in Rome on Palm Sunday.

40. Everyone who spoke to him in Rome, knowing that he had no money to go to Jerusalem, tried to talk him out of his trip, offering him all kinds of reasons why it would be impossible for him to find a free passage. But he felt a firm certainty within his soul that he would find a way of going to Jerusalem, and of this he had no doubt. After he had re-

The *quattrini* that Ignatius collected were coins of the lowest denomination then in use in Italy. The usual route from Gaeta to Rome went through Velletri, and the distance was about seventy-five miles. Since Ignatius arrived in Rome on Palm Sunday, we have a definite date for his entrance into the Eternal City. In 1523 Palm Sunday was celebrated on March 29.

40. It was customary for pilgrims to the Holy Land first to receive the pope's permission and benediction before starting out. Ignatius received his permission on March 31, two days after his arrival in Rome. A record of this permission, recently discovered, is preserved in the Vatican Archives, and Ignatius is there referred to as "Iñigo of Loyola, cleric of the Diocese of Pamplona".[2] When Pope Hadrian VI, a Dutchman and for-

---

[2] "Enecus de Loyola, clericus pampilonensis diocesis" (*FD*, doc. 64.). This document, discovered only in 1953 or 1954, was first published in 1956. See P. de Leturia and M. Battlori, "Documenta duo vaticana de familia Loyola atque de sancto Ignatio", *Archivum Historicum Societatis Iesu* 25 (1956): 26.

ceived the blessing of Pope Hadrian VI, he then set out for Venice, some eight or nine days after the feast of the Resurrection. He also took with him six or seven ducats, which he had received for his passage from Venice to Jerusalem, and these he had accepted only because he was overcome by the fear they had implanted in him by saying that there was absolutely no other way of getting there. Two days after leaving Rome he began thinking that this showed a lack of confidence in God, and the taking of those ducats so disturbed him that he thought it would be good to be finished with them. He decided, in the end, to give them with open hands to those he might meet on the way, who were usually the

mer tutor of Charles V, was elected to the Chair of Saint Peter on January 9, 1522, he had been residing in Spain and had been that country's prime minister. He arrived in Rome in August of that year, several months before Ignatius visited the city, and was to die on September 4, 1523, five months after Ignatius left the city.

The friends with whom Ignatius talked in Rome were most probably Spaniards, whom he met in the Spanish district of Rome near today's Piazza Navona,[3] and it was probably these friends who had taken up a collection among themselves and had given him a gift of several ducats to help defray the expenses of his passage to Jerusalem. These ducats were but a beginning toward the amount he would need for his passage; nevertheless, he felt that even having these few ducats was a denial of his former hope that God would get him there. Ignatius spent Holy Week in Rome, and during his two-week stay he surely visited the city's major basilicas. Since Easter that year fell on April 5, and since Ignatius informs us that he left Rome eight or nine days later, it would then seem that he began his journey to Venice about April 13 or 14.

---

[3] The Spanish hospice was next to the church of San Giacomo degli Spagnuoli, founded by Alfonso Paradiñas (d. 1485), canon of the cathedral of Seville and later Bishop of Ciudad Rodrigo (GV 241). The building was begun in 1450 and completed in 1478. The church now bears the name Nostra Signora del Sacro Cuore.

poor. This he did in such a way that when he arrived in Venice he had only a few *quattrini* with him, and those he needed for that night.

41. On his way to Venice, he slept outside under arches because of the restrictions then in force due to the plague. Once it happened that one morning as he was getting up he bumped into a man who, as soon as he saw him, fled in great fright because he must have had a very pale look about him.

Walking, he reached Chioggia, and from some of the companions who had joined him he learned that they would not be allowed to enter Venice. The companions decided to go to Padua and there get health certificates, and so he went along with them. Since he could not walk as they did—they were walking at a quick pace—they left him in a large field as night was coming on. While in the field Christ appeared to him in the way He usually appeared to him, as we have already stated, and this brought him great comfort. The next morning, still experiencing this consolation, he arrived at Padua's gates, and without forging any certificate, as I believe his companions had done, he entered the city without the guards asking anything of him. The same thing happened

41. The route that Ignatius followed from Rome to Venice is not known, but the more likely route was to pass through the cities of Narni, Terni, Spoleto, then head for Ancona on the coast, and then turn northward, passing through Rimini, Ravenna, Ferrara, and finally Chioggia, which is located at the entrance of the lagoon and only some fifteen miles from Venice.[4] Ignatius' vision of Christ in the field near Padua was similar to the visions he had had in Manresa (see no. 29) and was granted him to indicate that his pilgrimage was under our Lord's protection and that he need not worry about minor details such as health certificates and money for passage.

---

[4] See *PY* 116 n. 22; *GV* 243.

as he left the city, and this especially surprised his companions, since they had come to procure these certificates in order to go to Venice, while he showed no interest in getting one for himself.

42. When they arrived in Venice, inspectors came to the boat to check everyone, one by one, as many as were on board. But they left him alone. In Venice he supported himself by begging, and he slept in Saint Mark's Square. He did not want to go to the residence of the emperor's ambassador, nor did he make any special effort to find the means to pay for his passage. He enjoyed a great certainty of soul that God would provide the means for getting to Jerusalem, and this feeling so strengthened his resolve that no reason or fear suggested to him could make him waver.

One day, he came across a rich Spaniard who asked him what he was doing there and where he wanted to go. Learning of his plans, the Spaniard took him home for a meal and then kept him there for some days until his departure was

42. After a four-week walk and a short boat trip, Ignatius arrived in Venice about mid-May 1523. Because Venice, the capital of the Most Serene Republic, was an important seaport and had control over the Adriatic and a good portion of the Mediterranean, it was she that handled the pilgrim trade to the Holy Land. Upon Ignatius' arrival he spent his first night in a hospice, but the following nights he slept under the pillared colonnades of Saint Mark's Square. Since his trust was entirely in God, he saw no need to seek help from the Spanish ambassador, who at that time was Alonso Sánchez. The kind Spaniard who took Ignatius into his home until his departure for Jerusalem remains unknown.[5] While in Venice Ignatius, like the other pilgrims in the city, participated as per custom in the Corpus Christi procession and festivities, which fell that year on June 4.[6]

---

[5] See *OC* 114 n. 9; *FN* 1:418–20.

[6] See *GV* 244.

arranged. Ever since his days in Manresa the pilgrim had had the custom, when he was eating with others, of never talking at table, except to give brief answers. But he listened to all that was said and mentally noted certain items that he would later use in speaking about God. When the meal was over, he then joined in the conversation.

43. For this reason the good man and his entire household grew so fond of him that they desired him to stay with them and tried to keep him there. His host took him to the doge of Venice so that he could speak with him, that is, he arranged an entry and an audience with him. The doge listened to the pilgrim and gave instructions that he be given passage on the ship taking the governors to Cyprus.

Though many pilgrims had come that year on their way to Jerusalem, most of them had returned to their homeland because of the recent capture of Rhodes. Still, there were thirteen on the pilgrim ship, which was the first to depart, and eight or nine others waited for the governors' ship. While

43. The doge who gave Ignatius free passage to Cyprus was Andrea Gritti (1455–1538), who had been elected to that office on May 10, 1523,[7] just four days before Ignatius arrived in Venice. Because of the fall of Rhodes to the Turks in late December 1522, there were only twenty-one pilgrims in the city,[8] and since this number was much too small for the scheduled *Pilgrim Galley* to set sail, the pilgrims were placed on two merchant vessels. Thirteen were put aboard the smaller of the two, which Ignatius calls the "pilgrim ship", while the remaining eight, including our pilgrim, were on the *Negrona*. Since the island of Cyprus had but recently come under the control of Venice, the new governor,

---

[7] See *FN* 1:420 n. 10; *OC* 115 n. 10.

[8] Many of the pilgrims who had gathered in Venice, on hearing the news of the fall of Rhodes, returned home. Thus only a very small number remained. Five years previously, in 1518, the *Pilgrim Galley* carried more than two hundred pilgrims to the Holy Land (see *GP* 271).

waiting to set sail, a very high fever struck our pilgrim, and after it had made him quite ill for a few days, it then left him. The ship set sail the very day that he had taken a purgative. Those of the household asked the physician if he would be able to embark for Jerusalem, and the physician answered that he certainly could leave for Jerusalem to be buried there. That day he boarded ship and set sail; he vomited a great deal, but found himself relieved, and soon he was on the road to recovery. On that ship some individuals engaged in openly lewd and obscene behavior, which he severely condemned.

44. The Spaniards traveling with him advised him not to speak out, because the crew was considering depositing him on some island or other. But our Lord saw to it that they

Nicolò Dolfin,[9] was on his way to the island. The pilgrim ship set sail on June 29, 1523,[10] and the *Negrona* left Venice on July 14.[11]

44. Though Ignatius never kept a diary of his pilgrimage to the Holy Land,[12] two of the pilgrims on that 1523 journey did keep diaries, and

---

[9] See *GV* 247.

[10] See *OC* 115 n. 14.

[11] See *FN* 1:420 n. 10; *OC* 115 n. 10.

[12] Ignatius did write a letter from Jerusalem (see no. 46), addressed to Inés Pascual, in which he describes the voyage from Venice to the moment he was writing. The letter was three pages in length. Ribadeneira seems to have used it when writing Ignatius' biography (*FN* 1:1–4; *FN* 4:157). Both Juan Pascual and his daughter, Oriente Sagristá, testified to its contents during the beatification process. The letter was subsequently given to the Society, but then lost. See also Sebastián Bartina, "Tierra Santa en la vida y en la obra de San Ignacio de Loyola", *Razón y Fe* 158 (1958): 57. For a full description of what a pilgrimage to the Holy Land was like, see H. F. M. Prescott, *Friar Felix at Large: A Fifteenth-Century Pilgrimage to the Holy Land* (New Haven: Yale University Press, 1950). Friar Felix made two pilgrimages: one in 1480 and another in 1483. Though his pilgrimages preceded that of Ignatius by some forty years, nevertheless, the vicissitudes of the pilgrim in the Holy Land had hardly changed.

arrived speedily at Cyprus, where they left the ship and went overland to another port named Las Salinas, about ten leagues away. There they boarded the pilgrim ship, and he took nothing with him as rations except his confidence in God, just as he had done on the other ship. During this period our Lord appeared to him on many occasions, giving him much strength

from them we can construct a chronology. The diarists were Philip Hagen,[13] a gentleman from Strasbourg, aboard the pilgrim ship, and Peter Füssli,[14] a bell-founder from Zurich, aboard the *Negrona*. Besides Hagen on the pilgrim ship there was another German as well as eleven pilgrims from Brabant and from what is now the Netherlands. On the *Negrona*, in addition to Ignatius and Füssli, there were two more Swiss, a Tyrolese, and three Spaniards. Among the Spaniards were an unidentified priest, Diego Manes, Commander of the Order of Saint John, and his servant. For Ignatius to have remembered the commander's name after thirty years seems to indicate that he must have been sufficiently impressed by him. These were the Spaniards who kindly told Ignatius to close his eyes to the misbehavior taking place on the ship's deck. The *Negrona* carried a crew of thirty-two and many other passengers—government officials with their families and servants, as well as traders and merchants.

After leaving Venice the *Negrona* followed the Dalmatian coast, stopping at Rovigno (today's Rovinj, Croatia) and then in a bay near Pola to weather out a storm. On August 1 they glimpsed the port of Valona (now Vlorë, southern Albania) and on the third they passed the island of Zante (modern Zákinthos) and on the fifth that of Cerigo (Kithira). They then sailed past Rhodes on the eleventh and on the night of the thirteenth arrived at Cyprus. After a month at sea the *Negrona* docked at Famagusta

---

[13] Hagen's account was written in his Strasbourg dialect and was eventually published in *Vier Rheinische Palaestina-Pilgerschriften des XIV, XV und XVI Jahrhunderts*, ed. Ludwig Conrady (Wiesbaden, 1882), 233–89.

[14] Füssli's account was in his Swiss dialect and appeared as "Warhafte reiss gen Venedig und Ierusallem, beschen durch Peter Füssly und Heinrich Ziegler. Anno 1523", *Zürcher Taschenbuch* N.F. 7 (1884): 136–93. More recently it was again published as *Peter Füesslis Jerusalemfahrt 1523 und Brief über den Fall von Rhodes*, ed. L. M. Uffer (Zurich, 1982).

and consolation. It seemed to him that he saw a large round object, as though it were of gold, and this frequently appeared to him from the time they left Cyprus to the time they arrived at Jaffa. Making their way to Jerusalem on small donkeys, as was the custom, a Spaniard, a nobleman by his appearance, named Diego Manes, about two miles outside

on August 14, and there the governor disembarked. Benedetto Ragazzoni, the ship's captain, was scheduled to continue the voyage to Beirut, and the eight pilgrims were to disembark there and travel overland down to Galilee and then southward to Jerusalem. But because of the plague then afflicting Beirut, Ragazzoni ended his voyage at Famagusta. Consequently, the eight pilgrims had to leave the *Negrona* and walk the thirty miles to Las Salinas (modern Larnaca), where they met the pilgrim ship that had left Venice two weeks before them. At first Captain Jacopo Alberto was of a mind to abandon his thirteen pilgrims in Cyprus, but when the additional eight arrived from the *Negrona*, and after they had agreed to pay twenty ducats each for passage to Jaffa with return to Cyprus, Alberto agreed to take them aboard. Since the captain was making a profit on this deal, he gave Ignatius free passage, and the pilgrim ship set sail on August 19.

According to the diarists, the vessel came into sight of Jaffa on August 22, but because of a pilot's error they went farther south and then, delayed by contrary winds, did not put into Jaffa until August 25, a Tuesday. Now that they were in the Holy Land, the pilgrims gathered on deck and sang the *Te Deum* as well as the *Salve Regina*. Before the pilgrims were able to disembark, the captain had first to go to Ramle to inform the Franciscan friars, who had charge of the Holy Places, that the pilgrims had arrived, and also to Jerusalem to request a safe conduct and a Turkish escort for them. On August 31 the captain returned with two Franciscan guides and one hundred Turkish soldiers as escort.[15] Before leaving the ship the pilgrims were addressed by Friar Hugo, who spoke in German, Italian, and Latin. Since Ignatius knew none of these languages, we presume that it was the Spanish priest in the group who served as his interpreter.

---

[15] See *GP* 675.

Jerusalem devoutly suggested to the pilgrims that since they would shortly be arriving at the point where they would be able to see the Holy City, it would be good for all of them to prepare their consciences and proceed in silence.

45. Since this seemed agreeable to all, each one recollected himself, and a little before they arrived at the place whence they could get a glimpse of the city, they dismounted because they noticed friars waiting for them with a cross. When the pilgrim did see the city, he experienced great consolation, and all the others affirmed the same, saying that they all felt a joy that did not seem natural. He felt this same devotion on all his visits to the Holy Places.

He made a firm decision to remain in Jerusalem, constantly visiting the Holy Places. In addition to this devout

The twenty-one pilgrims set foot in the Holy Land on September 1 and immediately underwent a form of registration to ensure that no pilgrim would remain in Jerusalem.[16] Though the distance from Jaffa to Jerusalem is only thirty-three miles, the pilgrims were not to arrive for another three days. Mounted on donkeys, the pilgrims made their way to Ramle, where they spent the night.[17] Instead of leaving for Jerusalem the following day, they learned that they had to wait for a caravan of Jewish merchants coming from Cairo. The caravan finally arrived, and late on September 3, they started for the Holy City. As was customary, they traveled at night to avoid the day's heat.

45. The pilgrims had their first sight of Jerusalem at 10 A.M., Friday, September 4,[18] and entering the city through the Jaffa Gate, they were housed near the Church of the Holy Sepulcher in the Hospital of Saint John, the usual residence for pilgrims. The following day, September 5, with their Franciscan guide, the pilgrims followed the traditional itinerary in visiting the Holy Places in Jerusalem, for instance, Mass in the Upper

---

[16] See *GP* 676.

[17] The hospice in which they stayed in Ramle was built for Christian pilgrims by Philippe de Bourgogne in 1420 (*GP* 676).

[18] See *GP* 679.

desire of his, he was also intent on helping souls, and for this purpose he had with him letters of recommendation to the guardian. Handing them over to him, he informed the guardian of his intention to remain there because of his devotion,

Room, where our Lord washed the feet of His disciples, Mount Sion, the column of the flagellation, the Convent of the Dormition of Our Lady as well as the Church of the Holy Sepulcher, where they spent the entire night in prayer. On the sixth, a Sunday, they attended Mass in the edicule known as the Chapel of the Resurrection within that church, and that afternoon they retraced Christ's steps on his way to Calvary, but in reverse order, starting with the sepulcher and ending with Pilate's palace and the "Ecce Homo" arch.

On the seventh they once more had Mass in the Cenacle,[19] then they went down to the Kedron, to the tomb of Absalom, and entered the Garden of Olives. Off to Bethany, where they visited the house of Simon the Leper and the tomb of Lazarus. On their return they stopped at the Chapel of the Ascension and finally at the Grotto of Gethsemane, the site of Christ's agony. On the eighth they traveled by donkey to Bethlehem, prayed in the Basilica of the Nativity, and saw the Chapel of Saint Catherine as well as Saint Jerome's cell. That night was spent in prayer in the basilica. On the following day, the ninth, after Mass in the Grotto of the Nativity, they went to Ain Karim, where Mary visited her cousin Elizabeth. They returned to Jerusalem that evening.

The tenth was spent viewing the valley of Jehoshaphat, the brook Kedron, Siloe, the Garden of Olives, and the Tomb of the Virgin. That afternoon they went to the residences of Caiaphas and Annas, now converted into chapels. On the eleventh, Friar Hugo pointed out to the pilgrims the cave where David was said to have written and prayed the penitential psalms. There followed a reception with the Franciscan tertiaries at which the pilgrims were given mementoes of their pilgrimage. That night they again spent in the Church of the Holy Sepulcher.

September 12 and 13 were days of rest and on the afternoon of the fourteenth they again went to Bethany and stopped at the House of

---

[19] This Mass was one of the last Masses to be celebrated in the Cenacle, for in January 1524 the Muslims expelled the Franciscans from the site (*GP* 680).

but said nothing of his other desire to help souls. He often and openly spoke to others about his wanting to remain, but to no one did he mention his second desire. The guardian replied that he did not see how he could possibly stay since the convent was in such dire need that it could not even support the friars living there, and that was why he had determined to send some of them back home together with the pilgrims. The pilgrim answered that he wanted nothing from the convent but only that when he should come there for confession, they would hear him. This the guardian said he could do, but he would have to wait until the provincial (I think he was the head of the order in that country) returned from visiting Bethlehem.

Zechariah. On the fifteenth they visited Jericho and then went down to the Jordan, where some took baths and where everyone drank of its water. On their return some wanted to climb the Mount of the Temptation, but the Turkish escort would not hear of it. Because some four to five hundred Turkish cavalry arrived in Jerusalem from Damascus on September 16, the pilgrims were advised not to appear in the streets, and, thus, they remained in relative seclusion until September 20.[20] The night of the twenty-first was again spent in the Church of the Holy Sepulcher, and on the morning of the twenty-second three of the pilgrims were made Knights of the Holy Sepulcher.[21]

Sometime during his stay in Jerusalem, Ignatius visited the Guardian of the Franciscan monastery of Mount Sion[22] and made known to him his desire to remain behind. The Father Guardian, the local superior, felt that he himself could not grant the pilgrim that permission and said that it would have to wait until the provincial returned from Bethlehem.

---

[20] See *FN* 1:422 n. 11; *PY* 124–31; *IL* 83–84.

[21] See *GP* 682.

[22] At this time the Franciscan superior in Jerusalem was Jacques de Portu (*GP* 675).

46. Finding assurance in this promise, the pilgrim began writing letters to spiritual persons in Barcelona. After he had written one and was in the process of writing another—it was the eve of the pilgrims' departure—he was summoned by the guardian and the provincial, who had just returned. The provincial told him most kindly that he knew of his good intentions to remain in the Holy Places and that he had given much thought to this matter; nevertheless, because of his experience with others he judged that it was not a good idea. Many others had had the same desire, and some of them had been taken prisoner and some of them had been killed; his religious order was later obliged to ransom those in captivity. Therefore, he should be ready to leave with the other pilgrims on the following day. He replied that his decision to remain was fixed and that nothing could prevent him from carrying it out. With great honesty he gave the provincial to understand that though the provincial did not agree with him, and since this was not a matter that obliged under sin, he would not renounce his plans out of fear. In answer to him the provincial said that they had authority from the Apostolic See to expel or to keep anyone they chose and to excommunicate anyone who refused to obey, and in

46–48. The call to visit the Franciscan provincial came on September 22, immediately after Ignatius had finished one letter and was beginning a second. The first letter was undoubtedly the one that Inés Pascual received, describing Ignatius' pilgrimage, but which is no longer extant.[23] Once Ignatius heard that the provincial[24] possessed full authority, granted

[23] See n. 12 above.

[24] It is unclear who was acting as provincial in Jerusalem at this time. Angelo de Ferrata was appointed to the post on May 24, 1523, but it seems that he did not reach the Holy Land until sometime in 1524 (*GV* 252 n. 33).

his case they were of the opinion that he should not remain, and so forth.

47. The provincial was willing to show him the bulls empowering them to excommunicate, but he said he had no need to see them since he believed their reverences, and since they arrived at their decision in accordance with the authority they possessed, he would obey them. When this was all over he returned to the place where he was staying. Since it was not our Lord's will for him to remain in the Holy Places, a burning desire took hold of him to make a return visit to the Mount of Olives before leaving. On the Mount of Olives there is a stone from which our Lord ascended into heaven, and his footprints are still visible there. This was what he again wanted to see. Thus, without saying anything, and without taking a guide (for those who go about without a Turk as guide run great risks), he slipped away from the others and went by himself to the Mount of Olives. The guards there did not want to let him enter, but he gave them a penknife that he had with him. After he had said his prayers with heartfelt consolation, he got the desire to go to Bethphage. While there he remembered that on the Mount of Olives he had not taken full notice of the direction in which the right foot was pointing and which way the left. On his return there he gave his scissors, I think, to the guards so that they would let him enter.

48. When the monastery learned that he had left without a guide, the friars made every effort to find him. As he was

---

him by Rome, to determine who could remain in Jerusalem, our pilgrim immediately obeyed. But now that he would have to depart, he revisited the Mount of Olives. The stone from which our Lord ascended into heaven is still preserved there; the print of the left foot has been almost entirely coming down from the Mount of Olives he met a Christian of the Girdle who worked at the monastery, The Christian was carrying a large staff and, showing his great annoyance, waved it as if he were about to beat him up. When he came up to him, the servant vigorously grabbed him by the arm, and he let himself be led away easily. The good man never let him go. As he was going along the road, held tightly by the Christian, our Lord granted him great consolation, and it seemed to him that he saw Christ above him the whole way. This consolation remained with him in great measure until he arrived at the monastery.

erased by the devout kisses of pilgrims, but that of the right foot is still somewhat clear.[25] The servant whom the Franciscans sent looking for Ignatius presumably wore a special belt.[26] Having returned to the hospice, Ignatius prepared to leave the Holy Land.

---

[25] See *PY* 131 n. 38.

[26] *OC* 118 n. 21 states that the Christians of the Girdle was the name given to Syrian Christians who worked at the Franciscan monastery of Mount Sion in Jerusalem. The exact origin of this phrase seems to be lost. It would seem that the girdle they wore somehow identified them as Christians. *GV* 253 n. 36 suggests that the Syrian Christians were so called because at the time of their baptism, the priest conferring the sacrament used a cincture to bind the newly baptized. The phrase was still in use in 1922, for H. Vincent and F.-M. Abel record that these Christians wear a woolen cincture around their long tunics and that they are distinguished from non-Christians by the blue turban they wear (*Jérusalem. Recherches de topographie, d'archéologie et d'histoire* 2: *Jérusalem nouvelle* [Paris: Gabalda, 1922], 985). Prescott (*Friar Felix at Large* p. 190) speaks of Christians of the Girdle but does not distinguish them by the girdle they wear, but says, "The Christians of the Girdle dress in Saracen fashion except that, instead of the white turban, they wear one of bright or dark blue."

Chapter 5

Cyprus—Genoa: The Pilgrim's Return

(September 23, 1523–February 1524)

49. They set out the next day, and after arriving in Cyprus the pilgrims separated, boarding different ships. There were three or four ships in port going to Venice; one was Turkish, another was a very small vessel, and the third was splendid and sturdy and was owned by a wealthy Venetian. Some pilgrims asked the shipmaster of this last ship if he would be willing to take the pilgrim on board, but learning that he had no money he would not, though many begged him to

49. The pilgrims left Jerusalem on the night of September 23, 1523. On their way to Ramle they were attacked by bedouins who stole their food, and when they arrived bandit Turks locked them up for three days without food or water. The group finally reached Jaffa on October 2, and on the following day the pilgrims boarded ship and were on their way to Cyprus, landing at Las Salinas on the fourteenth.[1]

Since the *Negrona*, the vessel that had brought them to Cyprus, had already left, the pilgrims were forced to seek alternate means of returning to Venice. Ignatius' companions tried to get him passage on the large Venetian ship then in port, but its shipmaster retorted that if he were that holy he should travel as Saint James had traveled. Legend has it that after the saint's death in Jerusalem his body was placed on a ship that miracu-

[1]See *FN* 1:428 n. 1; *PY* 133.

do so and spoke highly of the pilgrim. The shipmaster answered that if he were a saint he could travel as Saint James traveled, or something similar. These same petitioners easily received a favorable response from the master of the small ship. They set sail one day in the morning, with a good wind, but by afternoon a storm rose, and the ships were scattered. The large vessel was lost off the island of Cyprus, and only its passengers were saved, while the Turkish ship and all passengers went down in the same storm. The small ship underwent much difficulty, but, finally it touched land in Apulia. It was when winter was at its worst, with snow and freezing temperatures. The pilgrim had no clothes other than a pair of breeches of rough cloth reaching to his knees, with his legs left bare. He had shoes and a doublet of black material,

lously spread its sails and took the body to northern Spain, thus explaining how the apostle's body arrived in Santiago de Compostela.[2]

While Ignatius was given free passage on the small ship, whose name has not been preserved, the diarists Füssli and Hagen had passage on the large vessel, and since Ignatius was no longer in their company the diaries that both men kept of their homeward voyage are no longer helpful to us.[3] Of the three ships that set sail for Venice in early November, only the small one returned there. The unusually long voyage of two and a half months would indicate that the vessel met storms and squalls on its journey. Ignatius merely says that the vessel had met with difficulty and the stopover on Italy's eastern shore was due to bad weather.

---

[2] See Jacobus de Voragine, *The Golden Legend: Readings on the Saints* (Princeton: Princeton University Press, 1993) 2:5.

[3] Here we follow the opinion of C. Dalmases as found in *FN* 1:428 n. 1. Some authors, e.g., Dudon (*IL* 85–88), have Ignatius traveling with Füssli, and, thus, they describe in detail the storm the *Malipiera* encountered and the ports where it sought refuge. There is one fact these authors fail to consider, namely, Ignatius explicitly states that his ship landed in Apulia, but the Füssli account has no mention of any landing in Apulia. Furthermore, Ignatius calls his vessel small, while the *Malipiera* was certainly not small.

torn at the shoulders, and a short loose coat that was threadbare.

50. He arrived in Venice in mid-January 1524, having been at sea, since leaving Cyprus, the entire months of November and December and half of January. In Venice he met one of the two gentlemen who had taken him into their homes before he departed for Jerusalem. The gentleman gave him an alms of fifteen or sixteen *giulii* and a piece of cloth that he folded several times and placed over his abdomen because of the severe cold.

After the said pilgrim came to realize that it was God's will that he not remain in Jerusalem, he kept wondering what he ought to do, and finally he was inclined toward spending some time in studies in order to help souls; and so he decided to go to Barcelona. Thus he left Venice for Genoa. One day, while in Ferrara's main church, finishing his devotions, a poor man asked him for an alms, and he gave him a *marchetto*, that is, a coin worth five or six *quattrini* After him another poor man came, and he also gave him a small coin but of greater value. Then to a third, having only *giulii* left, he gave him a *giulio*. When the poor people saw him dis-

50. Upon Ignatius' return to Venice, he met one of the two gentlemen who had befriended him prior to his going to the Holy Land. This gentleman is usually identified as Marcantonio Trevisano, a Venetian senator, whose palace was behind Saint Mark's Basilica.[4] The *giulii* that he gave Ignatius were silver coins minted during the pontificate of Pope Julius II (1503–1513) and still in circulation, each worth about one-tenth of a ducat. Ignatius spent two weeks in Venice considering what he ought to do with his life. He could still help others, but to be of greater assistance he determined that he should do some studying, and, thus, he decided to go to

---

[4] See *FN* 2:433 n. 29; *OC* 114 n. 7 and 9. In no. 42 Ignatius mentions but one Spaniard who befriended him in Venice.

pensing alms, they kept on coming until he gave away all that he had. Finally, many poor people came in a group requesting alms, but he asked their pardon saying he had nothing left.

51. Then he left Ferrara for Genoa. On the way he met some Spanish soldiers who treated him well that night. They were quite surprised that he was traveling that road because it passed almost in the exact middle between the French and imperial armies. The soldiers suggested that he leave the highway and take another and safer road, which they pointed out to him, but he did not follow their advice. Walking straight ahead on the same road, he came upon a town that had been burned and destroyed, and until that night he found no one to give him anything to eat. At sunset he came to a walled town where the guards immediately seized him, thinking he was a spy. They put him in a small hut next to the town's gate and questioned him, as they usually did those whom they suspected. He answered all their questions, saying that he knew nothing. They stripped him and searched his entire

Barcelona. He left Venice in early February, and was soon in Ferrara, where, while he was praying in the Cathedral of Saint George, beggars approached him for alms and with his usual generosity he gave away all that he had, leaving himself poorer than those who had sought his assistance.

51–53. Among the various incidents that happened during Ignatius' journey from Ferrara to Genoa, three remained in his memory. France and Spain were at war in a dispute over Milan, but in early 1524, when Ignatius was crossing through Lombardy, hostilities were fortunately at a standstill. At some unknown location Ignatius encountered Spanish soldiers; recognizing the traveler as a fellow countryman, the soldiers helped him in every way they could and even told him what road to follow to avoid the French. But Ignatius, preferring to place his confidence in God, purposely continued on the highway. He walked all day, and that evening he was seized as a spy, searched, and interrogated. Ignatius found spiritual consolation in this incident, for now he had the chance to imitate his body down to his shoes, to see if he were carrying any letters. Unable to learn anything by these means, they bound him in order to take him to their captain, who would make him talk. He asked that they take him wearing his coat, but they refused to give it to him and took him only in his breeches and doublet, which were mentioned earlier.

52. While on his way, the pilgrim had a representation of how Christ was led away, but this was not a vision as the others were. He was led down three main streets, and went without sadness but with joy and satisfaction. He was in the habit of addressing all whom he met in the familiar "you" form, and he kept to this practice because it was in this way that Christ and the apostles spoke, and so forth. Passing through these streets, the thought came to him, together with thoughts of the torture they could inflict on him, that it would be good for him to drop that custom on this occasion and speak to the captain in the more formal and polite manner. But he immediately perceived that this was a temptation and said: "Since it is, I will not speak to him in the formal and dignified manner, nor will I show him any mark of respect, nor will I take my cap off to him."

53. When they came to the captain's quarters, they left him in a lower room, and in a little while the captain came and spoke with him. Without showing any mark of courtesy, he answered in few words with long pauses between them. The captain took him for a madman and instructed those who had brought him in: "This man has no brains;

Master, who had also been arrested. Set free, Ignatius was soon again apprehended, but because the French captain was also a Basque, he permitted Ignatius to continue on his way.

When Ignatius arrived in Genoa, God's providence in his behalf was again made manifest. He unexpectedly came upon Rodrigo Portuondo, captain give him his belongings and throw him out." Leaving the residence, he soon met a Spaniard who lived in that city and who took him home and gave him something to eat, after many hours of not eating, and all that he needed for the night. When morning came he set out and walked until late afternoon, when two soldiers in a tower noticed him and came down to apprehend him. They led him to their captain, who was a Frenchman. The captain asked him, among other things, from what country he came, and learning that he came from Guipúzcoa, he said: "I come from near there", seemingly from the neighborhood of Bayonne, and he continued: "Take him, give him something to eat, and treat him kindly."

On this journey from Ferrara to Genoa, many other less interesting things happened, and finally he arrived in Genoa, where a Basque named Portundo recognized him. On many occasions he had spoken to him when the pilgrim served at the court of the Catholic King. This man secured passage for him on a ship going to Barcelona and which ran great danger of being captured by Andrea Doria, who was then in the service of the French and who had given them chase.

general of the Spanish galleys.[5] Ignatius had known him since his days when he was in the retinue of the royal treasurer Velázquez de Cuéllar and had met him when the treasurer visited the royal court.[6] Portuondo easily arranged for Ignatius to board one of the ships going to Barcelona, and though Andrea Doria, the famous Genoese admiral—now serving the French king—pursued the Spanish vessel, he failed to capture it.

---

[5] Though the text gives his name as Portundo, it was actually Portuondo. See *OC* 121 n. 8.

[6] See F. de Borja de Medina, "Íñigo López de Loyola: Probable estancia en Sevilla (1508 y 1511) y su reflejo en los Ejercicios", *Archivum Historicum Societatis Iesu* 63 (1994): 20–29.

Chapter 6

Barcelona and Alcalá: Student Days

(February/March 1524–June 21, 1527)

54. After he had arrived in Barcelona, he informed Isabel Roser and Master Ardévol, who was then teaching grammar, of his desire to study. The idea seemed good to both of them; he offered to teach him without charge, and she offered to supply him with whatever he needed to support himself. The pilgrim knew a friar in Manresa, I think of the order of Saint Bernard, a very spiritual man, and he wished to stay with him in order to learn how he could more easily give himself to the spirit and how to be of help to souls. So he answered that he would accept their offer if in Manresa he did not find the spiritual profit he hoped to find. When he went there he found that the friar had died, and returning to Barcelona, he began his studies with great diligence. But one thing was proving a great hindrance to him, and that

54–55. Ignatius asserts (see no. 57) that he arrived in Barcelona during Lent 1524. That year Ash Wednesday was on February 9,[1] and since he had departed Venice sometime at the beginning of February, had walked across northern Italy, and had taken a ship to Barcelona, he probably

---

[1]See *OC* 121 n. 1; however, *FN* 1:440 n. 8 says that Lent began on February 10.

was that whenever he tried to memorize anything, as is necessary in the early stages of grammar study, new understand-
ings of spiritual things and new delights came to him, and in
such a way that he could neither memorize anything nor
could he rid himself of them, no matter how much he tried.

55. Giving much thought to this matter, he said to himself: "Even when I am at prayer at Mass, such clear under-
standings do not come to me!" Then, little by little, he came
to recognize that these were temptations. After saying a prayer,
he went to Our Lady of the Sea, near his teacher's house,
having asked him to meet him in the church and hear him
out. While they were seated together, he faithfully described

arrived in that city in the latter part of February or early March. He renewed his acquaintance with Isabel Roser,[2] and it was she who introduced him to Master Jerónimo Ardévol. The studies that Ignatius especially
wanted to pursue were in Christian perfection, and with this in mind he
went to Manresa to put himself under the tutelage of a monk he had
previously known at the Cistercian monastery of Saint Paul the Hermit.[3]
Having learned that the monk had died, Ignatius returned to Barcelona
and accepted the assistance that Roser and Ardévol had offered him. In
the beginning Ardévol gave Ignatius private instruction, but when the
former accepted a position at the University of Barcelona, he invited Ignatius to sit in his classes—a thirty-four-year-old sitting among teenage

[2] She was Ignatius' benefactor, not only during his days in Barcelona, but
also later during his years of study in Paris. In 1543 she came to Rome, and on
December 25, 1545, she and two other ladies pronounced vows in the Society
of Jesus, but because of ensuing difficulties Ignatius dispensed her from those
vows nine months later. She returned to Barcelona in 1547 and entered the
Franciscan convent of Santa María de Jerusalén, where she died in 1554. For
further details, see *LW* 262–95.

[3] *IL* 94 suggests that this monk may have been Alfonso de Guerreto and
that he may have been a victim of the plague that desolated that area during
August-September of 1523. José M. March is of a different opinion in his
"Quién y de donde era el monje manresano, amigo de San Ignacio de Loyola",
Estudios Ecclesiasticos 4 (1925): 185–93.

to his teacher all that was going on in his soul, how little progress he had made until then, and for what reason. But he made a promise to his teacher, saying: "I promise you, that as long as I can find bread and water in Barcelona to support myself, I will never miss any of your classes during these two years." Since he made this promise with great earnestness, he never again had those temptations. The stomach pain, which he first had in Manresa and which was the reason why he wore shoes, now left him, and he found his stomach feeling as well as when he left for Jerusalem. This was the reason why, during his studies in Barcelona, the desire to resume his former penances returned to him. He made holes in the soles of his shoes and kept enlarging them little by

boys.[4] The rudiments of Latin did not come easily to Ignatius. When he tried to memorize its various declensions and conjugations, spiritual lights invaded his mind, pulling him away from his studies. But once he acknowledged that these came from the evil spirit, he was no longer troubled by them. With his usual openness, Ignatius spoke to his teacher about his lack of progress, but, now that he had discovered the cause of his problem, he promised to put forth his best efforts. The church of Our Lady of the Sea was located near the port and was also near Ardévol's residence.

During Ignatius' two years in Barcelona, he lodged with the widow Inés Pascual, whom he had met in Manresa and who had a little shop in Barcelona near the church of Our Lady of the Sea. Her living quarters were above the shop. Ignatius' room was there, but for his daily bread he went begging in the streets. He continued to devote a specified amount of time to prayer, and he likewise continued his practice of penance. But to disguise this fact he made holes in his shoes so that he could feel the rough cobblestones as he made his way through the city.

---

[4] Ardévol began teaching at the *Estudio General* in Barcelona in 1525. See *OC* 121 n. 3; *GV* 260–62; and C. Dalmases, S.J., "Los estudios de San Ignacio en Barcelona (1524–1526)", *Archivum Historicum Societatis Iesu* 10 (1941): 283–93.

little, so that when winter's cold came there was nothing there but the upper part of the shoes.

56. After he completed two years of study and after having been told that he had made great progress in them, his teacher told him that he was now ready to pursue the liberal arts and that he should go to Alcalá. Notwithstanding, he had a doctor in theology examine him, and he gave him the same advice. He set out alone for Alcalá, though I believe he already had some followers. Upon his arrival in Alcalá he began begging and living on alms. One day, after he had lived in this manner for some ten or twelve days, a cleric and others with him, seeing him begging, began to make fun of

---

56. After two years of basic Latin, Ignatius was prepared for advanced work, and so Master Ardévol suggested that he go to the University of Alcalá. During his stay in Barcelona Ignatius met three individuals who, like him, were interested in helping souls, and these three, Calixto da Sa,[5] Lope de Cáceres,[6] and Juan de Arteaga,[7] eventually followed him to Alcalá. Bidding good-bye to his friends, Ignatius started his three-hundred-mile walk sometime in July 1526.[8] Situated on the Henares river, Alcalá

---

[5] Calixto de Sa may have been born in Segovia. Before he attached himself to Ignatius he made a pilgrimage to the Holy Land, probably in 1524. After Ignatius went to Paris in 1528, Calixto intended to follow but then changed his mind. He twice visited Mexico and returned a wealthy man, settling down in Salamanca. See FN 1:171 n.10.

[6] Lope de Cáceres was born in Segovia and had been in the service of the Viceroy of Catalonia. After Ignatius moved to Paris, he returned to Segovia. See FN 1:1760 n. 9.

[7] Juan de Arteaga was born in Estepa and remained with Ignatius until the latter moved to Paris. In July 1540 Pope Paul III appointed him Bishop of Chiapas in Mexico. He arrived ill in Veracruz and went to Mexico City to recuperate, but he died there on September 8, 1541, and was buried in the city's cathedral. See FN 170 n. 8.

[8] See FN 1:440 n. 8; OC 123 n. 8.

him and uttered some insulting remarks, as it frequently happens when someone healthy is seen begging. At that moment the gentleman in charge of the new hospital of Antezana was passing by and, feeling sorry for him, called him over and took him to the hospital, where he gave him a room and all he needed.

57. He spent almost a year and a half studying in Alcalá; since he had arrived in Barcelona, where he studied for two years, during Lent 1524, he thus arrived in Alcalá in 1526. There he studied the dialectics of Soto, the physics of Albert,

---

was justly proud of its university, founded in 1508 by Cardinal Ximénez de Cisneros;[9] by 1526 it had become a renowned center of learning and humanism. Ignatius, as was his custom, supported himself by alms, and he tells of an incident when a cleric publicly ridiculed him for begging when he was neither unwell nor a cripple. In the eyes of the cleric, Ignatius was but a lazy vagrant; in his own eyes, begging was his way of manifesting his total dependence on God. Another passerby witnessed that encounter and noticed how meekly the beggar accepted the rebuke. Moved by this example of humility, the gentleman, who was the administrator of the Hospital of Our Lady of Mercy, also called Antezana after its founder,[10] offered Ignatius a place to live.

57. After the summer recess the university again opened its doors to its students. Though Ignatius mentions three courses that he followed, still his name does not appear on any of the known lists of students attending the university.[11] It appears more likely that he had no set plan of study, and thus he did not matriculate but attended whatever lectures he chose.

---

[9] Cisneros became Archbishop of Toledo in 1495, and as archbishop he financed the printing of many religious books, the most famous of which was the polyglot Bible, *Complutensis*, in six volumes (1514–1517). It contained the first printed text of the Greek New Testament. He died in 1517.

[10] The hospital was founded in 1483 by Luis de Antezana, a gentleman-in-waiting of their Catholic Majesties. The exact identity of the individual in question is uncertain, but he was either Lope de Deza or Juan Vázquez. See *FN* 1:439 n. 7; *OC* 123 n. 7; *GV* 271 n. 2.

[11] See *FN* 1:418 n. 5.

and the Master of the Sentences. While in Alcalá he engaged in giving the Spiritual Exercises and in explaining Christian doctrine, and by these means he brought forth fruit for the glory of God. Many people came to a deep knowledge of and a relish for spiritual things. Others were undergoing various trials, like the one who desired to scourge himself but was unable to, as if someone were holding back his

He says that he studied the logic of Soto,[12] the natural philosophy of Albert the Great,[13] and the theology of Peter Lombard[14]—a strange mixture of subjects for someone just entering the academic world. When not in the lecture halls, Ignatius was usually in the courtyard of the Antezana Hospital, teaching catechism to children or speaking to grown-ups about the commandments and the love of God and of neighbor. He likewise explained to his listeners different methods of prayer, ideas which he took from the notes he had made at Manresa and which eventually became the Spiritual Exercises.

Among the people Ignatius got to know in Alcalá there was one who was somewhat special to him, and that was Diego de Eguía.[15] Diego was

---

[12] Domingo Soto (1494–1560) had been professor at Alcalá before he entered the Dominican Order in 1524. His text on logic, *Summulae*, was first printed in Burgos in 1529, but an earlier manuscript version of it could have been in use in Alcalá when Ignatius was there. See *GV* 271–72.

[13] St. Albert the Great's (c. 1200–1280) *Physicorum libri VIII* was his extended commentary on Aristotle's natural philosophy and was written between 1245 and 1248.

[14] Peter Lombard's (c. 1095–1160) *Sententiarum libri IV* was completed about 1157. It was a systematic presentation of scholastic theology, and because the book had become the favorite theological text of the Middle Ages, Peter became familiarly known as the Master of the Sentences.

[15] The original text gives the family name as Guía. Diego de Eguía was born in Estella in Navarre and on his mother's side was related to Francis Xavier. He joined Ignatius in Venice in January 1537, pronounced his vows in Rome on February 22, 1542, and died there on June 16, 1556, just weeks before Ignatius' own death. Diego's brother Esteban also joined Ignatius in Venice in 1537, and he died in Rome on January 28, 1551. See *FN* 1:110 n. 3; *OC* 124 n. 13.

hand, and other such cases. All this gave rise to much talk in the city, especially because of the great number of people who gathered wherever he was explaining doctrine.

Shortly after coming to Alcalá, he got to know Don Diego de Eguía, who was then living with his brother, who had a printing business in Alcalá, and was rather well off. They gave him alms to help the poor and kept three of the pilgrim's companions in their house. Once, when he asked for alms for some needs he had, Don Diego said he had no money, but he opened a chest containing various items and gave him bed covers of different colors and some candlesticks and other similar things. The pilgrim wrapped them all in a sheet, put them on his shoulder, and went out to assist the poor.

58. As it was already said, rumors began flying throughout that region about the things happening in Alcalá; some individuals said one thing, while others said something else. This matter reached the Inquisition in Toledo, and when the

a priest and was living with his brother Miguel, a respected printer.[16] The Eguía brothers gave lodging to Ignatius' three companions when they first came from Barcelona and were very generous in supplying him with money and whatever he needed for the poor. In later years Diego entered the Society in Rome and for a time there served as Ignatius' confessor.

58–59. Because of the number of children and women who gathered to listen to Ignatius' instructions—a sight somewhat unusual in Alcalá—stories began to be spread about him, his companions, and their teaching. Since they all wore tunics made of sackcloth, they unwittingly gave the appearance of forming a special group. And since they were neither priests

---

[16] In 1525 and again in 1526 Miguel printed a Spanish translation of Erasmus' *Enchiridion militis christiani*, and it is probable that it was through these editions that Ignatius had his first contact with Erasmus. See *GV* 274–78.

inquisitors came to Alcalá the pilgrim was warned by their host, who told him that they were calling them "sack wearers" and "enlightened ones", I believe, and that they were going to make mincemeat of them. They immediately began

nor religious, but laymen involved in street preaching, some observers undoubtedly viewed them as part of a "reform movement", perhaps even influenced by the teachings of Martin Luther. Others thought they were *alumbrados*, that is, members of a Spanish religious movement who claimed direct illumination of the Holy Spirit and considered themselves exempt from the usual means of sanctification as proposed by the Church. Ignatius and his group thus came under suspicion, and news of their novel activity reached the Inquisition in Toledo.

Two inquisitors came to Alcalá,[17] and together with the archbishop's representative, Juan Rodríguez de Figueroa,[18] they formed the inquisitorial board. They met at the episcopal residence on November 19, 1526, and summoning four witnesses,[19] they questioned them about the manner of life Ignatius and his companions lived and what they taught. The result was that the examiners found nothing wrong with the group's way of life or anything erroneous in their teaching. Since none of the witnesses said anything negative about Ignatius, the board felt no need to summon him. The inquisitors then returned to Toledo and left it to Figueroa to inform Ignatius of its decision. This he did on November 21.[20] Since

---

[17] The two inquisitors were Dr. Miguel Carrasco, professor of theology at Alcalá, and Licentiate Alonso Mejía, a canon of Toledo. See *OC* 125 n. 17; *FN* 1:443 n. 18; *GV* 281.

[18] Figueroa was the Archbishop of Toledo's vicar general in Alcalá. Charles V later appointed him Regent of the Kingdom of Naples, and he served as President of the Council of Castile. He was always friendly toward Ignatius and died in Madrid on March 23, 1565.

[19] The witnesses were the Franciscan Friar Hernando Rubio, Beatriz Ramires, a pious lady, and María and Julián Martínez, both of whom worked at the Antezana Hospital. See *GV* 281–84.

[20] The documents of these Alcalá investigations may be found in *FD* 319–49. A very good resumé is in *PY* 158–62.

an examination and investigation into their lives, but in the end they returned to Toledo without summoning them, though they had come with that purpose in mind. They left the trial to the vicar Figueroa, who is now with the emperor. Several days later the vicar summoned them and informed them that an investigation and examination had been made into their lives by the inquisitors and that no error was found in their teaching or in their living habits, and, thus, they could continue doing what they were doing,

the board had found their life and teaching blameless, they were permitted to continue as they had been doing. However, since they did not belong to any religious order and because their tunics resembled a religious habit, they were to give them up and wear the customary clothing of clerics or laymen. Figueroa must have mitigated this portion of the board's decision, for rather than insisting that they get new clothing, he thought it sufficient if they merely dyed their clothes different colors so as not to appear as a group set apart. The Juanico[21] Ignatius here mentions was a young Frenchman whom he met at the Antezana Hospital.

Though the inquisitors had exonerated his group, Ignatius still wondered how beneficial such investigations actually were. Priests in the parishes could still refuse to permit them to receive weekly Communion. Ignatius tells how one of his companions had recently been refused Communion and that he himself received similar treatment. Before departing Alcalá, Ignatius sought assurance that there was nothing wrong in his actions nor error in his teaching. Figueroa replied that if there were heresy in Ignatius' teaching the inquisitors would certainly have discovered it and that they would have sentenced him to be burned. Knowing that the Inquisition was no respecter of persons, he retorted that even if heresy were found in the vicar's teaching, he too would suffer the same penalty. The tunics were dyed, and within a few weeks Figueroa asked Ignatius to cease going about barefoot and to wear shoes. He did not want Ignatius to have

---

[21] Jean Reynalde had been a page in the service of Martín de Córdoba, Viceroy of Navarre. He went to Alcalá to begin studies and, being wounded in a student brawl, was taken to the Antezana Hospital, where he got to know Ignatius. Upon recovery, he asked to become a member of Ignatius' group.

and without any restrictions. But since they were not members of a religious order, it did not seem proper for all of them to go about wearing a habit. It would be better, so he ordered, if two of them, here he pointed to the pilgrim and to Arteaga, were to dye their clothes black, and the other two, Calixto and Cáceres, to dye theirs a light brown. Juanico, who was a Frenchman, could remain as he was.

59. The pilgrim said that they would do as they were ordered. "But," he added, "I do not know how beneficial such investigations are. The other day a priest refused to give the Sacrament to one of us because he receives Communion every week, and they have made difficulties for me. We would like to know whether they have found any heresy in us." Figueroa answered: "No; if they had, they would have burned you." "They would have likewise burned you", the pilgrim retorted, "if they found heresy in you." They dyed their clothes as they had been ordered to do, and about two or three weeks later, Figueroa ordered the pilgrim to wear shoes and not go about barefoot. He obeyed quite peacefully, as he always did in such matters when commanded to do so.

anything in his manner of dress that could be interpreted as his being a monk or a religious.

On March 6, 1527, Figueroa initiated another investigation into Ignatius' teaching, but this was done on his own authority. Ignatius surmised that more denunciations had been brought against him, and perhaps the fact that a prominent lady had once come to visit him. The fact that she had been veiled and had come at a very early hour may have added to these suspicions. Figueroa summoned three witnesses, but from these he heard only praise for Ignatius and found nothing wrong in his teaching.[22]

---

[22] The woman who came at dawn remains unknown. The three witnesses who came to Ignatius' defense were the widow Mencia de Benavente, her sixteen-year-old daughter, Ana, and the sixteen-year-old Leonor, daughter of Ana de Mena. See *GV* 284-85.

Four months later, Figueroa himself again investigated them. In addition to the usual charges, I believe it also came about because a married woman of some prominence, who had a special interest in the pilgrim, came to the hospital one morning, at dawn, and in order not to be recognized wore a veil, as is the custom in Alcalá de Henares. When she entered the hospital, she removed her veil and went to the pilgrim's room. But they did nothing to them at that time, nor did they summon them after the investigation, nor did they say anything to them.

60. Another four months later—he was now living in a small building outside the hospital—a policeman one day came to his door and, calling out to him, said: "Come with me for a little while!" He put him in jail and said: "You are not to leave this place until you are ordered otherwise." It was then summer, and since he was not all that confined there, many people came to visit him, and he did the same there as when he was free; he gave instructions in doctrine and gave the Exercises. Though many lawyers and attorneys

60–61. Ignatius lived in relative peace for another four months, but then in the middle of Holy Week—either Holy Thursday or Good Friday (April 18 or 19)—he was unexpectedly taken to prison without knowing the reason. His freedom was not overly restricted, for friends still came to visit him, and he continued to give instructions and lead others through the Exercises. Among his friends were lawyers who offered to represent him, but he preferred to depend on God. He especially remembered the kindness of Doña Teresa Enríquez de Cárdenas,[23] who wanted to use her influence to have him released, but again Ignatius chose to remain there until God saw fit to liberate him.

---

[23] Her husband was the treasurer of Castile, and she was known for her charity and devotion to the Blessed Sacrament. See *GV* 286.

offered him their services, he refused them. He especially remembers Doña Teresa de Cárdenas, who sent someone to visit him and many times offered to have him released, but he wanted nothing, always saying: "He, for whose love I have come here, will set me free if His will is served thereby."

61. He was in prison for seventeen days without anyone interrogating him, or without his knowing the reason for his being there. At the end of this time, Figueroa came to the prison and questioned him about many matters, even asking if he encouraged others to observe Saturday. He asked if he knew two ladies in particular, who were mother and daughter, and to this he answered that he did. And if he had known anything of their departure before they had set out. He answered no, appealing to the oath he had taken. The vicar, placing his hand on his shoulder as a sign of his satisfaction, then said: "This was the reason why were you were brought here." Among the many people who followed the pilgrim

It was after seventeen days of confinement that Ignatius finally learned what had brought him there. Figueroa and a notary arrived on an official visit, with the notary recording all questions and answers. Of the many questions asked, Ignatius records only two. The question about Saturday was the vicar's indirect way of asking whether Ignatius was a Jewish convert. In Spain, at that time, many Jews underwent forced conversion, and though they acted as Christians externally, they secretly practiced their old religious rites. To the vicar's question, Ignatius replied that his Saturdays were spent in devotions to our Lady and that he had no other observances. In addition he added that there were no Jews living in Guipúzcoa, his homeland.[24] Figueroa then touched on the reason why Ignatius was in jail. A certain María del Vado and her daughter Luisa Velázquez, together with their servant Catalina, had suddenly disappeared from Alcalá.[25]

---

[24] *FN* 1:174.
[25] See *FN* 1:448 n. 26; *OC* 127 n. 26.

there were a mother and daughter, both widows, and the daughter was very young and beautiful, and both had made much progress in spiritual matters, but especially the daughter, and to such a degree that though they were noble ladies, they had gone on foot to the shrine of Veronica's veil in Jaén, alone and perhaps begging their way.

This caused much talk in Alcalá, and Dr. Ciruelo, who was somewhat responsible for them, thought that the prisoner had influenced them into going, and thus he had him arrested. In response to what the vicar had said, the prisoner answered: "Would you like me to speak a bit more on this matter?" "Yes", he replied. "Then you should be aware", said the prisoner, "that both these women had many times enthusiastically spoken to him about their desire to go through the world serving the poor in one or another hospital. I have always tried to steer them away from that plan because the daughter was so young, so attractive, and so on. I told them that whenever they wanted to visit the poor, they could do so right here in Alcalá, and they can also accompany the Most Blessed Sacrament." When this conversation ended, Figueroa left with his notary, who had written everything down.

Dr. Pedro Ciruelo, a professor at the university who acted as the ladies' protector, knowing that they had been in contact with Ignatius, presumed that he was responsible for their disappearance and consequently lodged a complaint with the vicar. The outcome was that a policeman led Ignatius to jail. Ignatius conceded that he knew the ladies but likewise added that, knowing of their desire to travel about to help the poor, he had tried to dissuade them by showing that they could aid the poor in their own city and that they could attend the priest as he carried Viaticum to the dying. Figueroa was genuinely satisfied with Ignatius' explanation, but the prisoner had to remain there until the ladies returned home to corroborate his story.

62. At that time Calixto was in Segovia, and hearing of his imprisonment, he came at once, though he had only recently recovered from a serious illness, and desired to be in jail with him. But the pilgrim told him that it would be better for him to go and present himself to the vicar, who treated him kindly and said that he would give the order for him to be imprisoned, for he too should remain there until the women returned to confirm the prisoner's story. Calixto spent several days in jail, but when the pilgrim saw that it

62–63. During the period when Ignatius was waiting for the devout ladies to return, Calixto, recovering from a grave illness in Segovia, heard of Ignatius' imprisonment and came to Alcalá to join him, but his already poor health only further deteriorated, and Ignatius arranged to have him released.

The ladies finally returned and presented themselves to Figueroa.[26] They explained that they had made a pilgrimage to Jaén in southern Spain to visit the shrine of the Holy Face and had then gone to Guadalupe to pray before a miraculous statue of our Lady.[27] They also confessed that their pilgrimage had been entirely their own doing and that Ignatius had had no part in their going. Figueroa's sentence was read to Ignatius by the notary on June 1. He was free, but he and his companions were to dress as the other students did and were forbidden to speak on matters of the faith until they had pursued further studies.[28] Of his little group Ignatius had the most education, but he had to admit that what he had was indeed very little. Since Figueroa's decision brought an end to his apostolate in Alcalá, Ignatius began to think of his future. Paramount in his thinking was his earnest desire to help souls, and with that in mind he determined to visit

---

[26] *FN* 1:448 n. 27 indicates that the ladies appeared before Figueroa on May 21, 1527. One wonders why the sentence freeing Ignatius was only given on June 1.

[27] See *FD* 340–42.

[28] Ignatius speaks of four years of study, but Figueroa's sentence demanded only three (see *FN* 1:450 n. 31).

was harming his bodily health—since he had not yet fully recovered—he got him released through the services of a physician who was a good friend of his.

Forty-two days had passed from the day the pilgrim went to prison to the day he was released. At the end of that period the two devout ladies returned, and the notary went to the prison to read him his sentence. He was free, but they were to dress as did the other students, and they were not to speak on matters of faith for the next four years until they had pursued further studies, for at present they were not sufficiently educated. It was the pilgrim, to tell the truth, who knew the most, but he had no solid foundation, and this was the first thing he usually mentioned when anyone examined him.

63. As a result of this decision he became a bit doubtful as to what he ought to do. It seemed to him that the door was now being closed on his helping souls, since they gave him no reason other than the fact that he had no formal studies. In the end he decided to go to Archbishop Fonseca of Toledo and put his case in his hands.

the Archbishop of Toledo, Alonso de Fonseca,[29] who was then at the royal court in Valladolid.

Ignatius left Alcalá in late June and had his conversation with the archbishop in early July. Now that Ignatius was in Valladolid, outside the archdiocese of Toledo, he told the archbishop that though he was no longer bound by the decision that Figueroa had passed in the archbishop's name,

---

[29] He became Archbishop of Toledo in 1524 and died in 1534. He was a great patron of learning and was an acquaintance of Erasmus, to whom he granted an annual pension of two hundred gold ducats. In return, Erasmus dedicated his edition of Augustine's works to him. The archbishop was visiting Valladolid for the baptism of the son of Charles V, the future Philip II, who had been born on May 21, 1527.

He left Alcalá and met the archbishop in Valladolid. He faithfully narrated what had happened and said that though he was no longer under the archbishop's jurisdiction, nor was he obliged to follow his decision, nevertheless, he would do whatever the archbishop commanded. He spoke to him in the same familiar manner that he used with everyone. The archbishop listened attentively and, realizing that he wanted to go to Salamanca, said that he had friends in Salamanca as well as a college and offered all this to him. As he was leaving, the archbishop gave him four *escudos*.

nevertheless, because of his goodwill he would still do whatever the archbishop should command after he had heard Ignatius' narration of the events of the past several months. When the archbishop heard the story he was impressed by Ignatius' sincerity, and sensing his genuine desire to help others, and to attend the University of Salamanca to pursue his studies further, the archbishop acquiesced. He told Ignatius that he had many friends in Salamanca and that he had founded the College of Saint James for poor students at the university, and all this he was willing to offer him.

Chapter 7

Salamanca: On Trial

(Mid-July–Mid-September 1527)

64. After his arrival in Salamanca and while he was praying in a church, a devout lady recognized him as being one
of the group, for his four companions had already been there
several days. She asked him his name and then took him to
the place where the companions were staying. When they
passed sentence in Alcalá that they were to dress as students,

---

64–65. While Ignatius was on his way to visit the Archbishop of Toledo
in Valladolid, his four companions left Alcalá for Salamanca. After his visit
with the Spanish prelate, Ignatius walked the seventy miles to be with his
friends once again. Salamanca was the home of Spain's most important
university, as famous as those of Paris and Oxford. Shortly after his arrival
in mid-July 1527, Ignatius was recognized by the clerical student dress he
was wearing. In Alcalá he and his companions were ordered to dress like
the other students, but since the students of Salamanca wore a style of
dress different from that of the students in Alcalá, Ignatius and companions, without intending to, stood out from among the others. A certain
woman, who had come to know Ignatius' group,[1] seeing that he was wear-

---

[1] In the Spanish text, the word we have translated as "group" is *compañía*.
This is somewhat interesting because *Compañía* is the name that Ignatius and
the first Jesuits chose as their name in 1537. Does this reference to his Alcalá-
Salamanca friends as a *compañía* indicate that Ignatius thought of these men as
the first beginnings of the *Compañía de Jesús*?

the pilgrim said: "When you ordered us to dye our clothes, that we did. But now we are not able to do what you ask since we do not have the resources to purchase new ones." Hence the vicar himself provided them with caps, clothing, and other student apparel, and thus dressed, they left Alcalá.

In Salamanca he went to confession to a friar of Saint Dominic in the church of San Esteban. One day, some ten or twelve days after his arrival, his confessor said to him: "The Fathers here in the house would like to speak with you." "In the name of God", he answered. The confessor then said: "It would be good if you would come and dine with us on Sunday, but I want to tell you in advance that they will want to know many things about you." So on Sunday he came with Calixto, and after dinner the subprior—the prior was absent—together with the confessor and, I believe, another friar, went

ing similar garb, surmised that he too was one of them. Thus, she approached him and took him to where his friends were staying.

Since Salamanca was outside the jurisdiction of the Archbishop of Toledo, the sentence passed on him in Alcalá was without force there, so Ignatius immediately set about his apostolate of gathering children for instruction and speaking to adults about God and prayer. This new and unheard-of activity was soon brought to the attention of the Dominican friars of San Esteban, a priory known as a center of learning and as the bulwark of orthodoxy in the city. Most of its friars were professors at the university.

Following his custom of weekly confession, Ignatius visited the church of San Esteban. There is nothing strange in his choice of a Dominican for his confessor; he had had one while in Manresa and had resided for a time in the Dominican monastery there. On his subsequent visit to his confessor—about two weeks after coming to the city—the priest informed Ignatius that the friars in his community were interested in him and that he was invited to dine with them on the following Sunday. The confessor's warning that the friars would grill him on his activities did not deter him from accepting the invitation. The following day Ignatius and Calixto had dinner with the friars, and afterward the subprior, Father Nicolás with them to a chapel. With all graciousness the subprior began to speak of the good reports they had received about their life and habits, and how they went about preaching like apostles, but they would now like to have more details on these matters. Thus he began by asking what studies had they done. The pilgrim answered: "Of all of us, I have studied the most", and then went on to give a clear account of the little he had studied and how limited that training was.

65. "Then, about what do you preach?" The pilgrim said: "We do not preach, we speak to a few in a friendly manner about the things of God, just as one does after dinner with those who invite us." "But," the friar asked, "of what godly things do you speak? That is precisely what we would like to know." The pilgrim answered: "Sometimes we speak about one virtue, then another, always with praise; sometimes we speak about one vice, then another, always condemning it." "You have had no education," the friar spoke out, "and you

de Santo Tomás,[2] together with two other friars, one of them being Ignatius' confessor, took their guests to a chapel. The subprior initiated the discussion by asking about their educational background. Ignatius admitted, as he had done in Alcalá, that his theological training was but a few disconnected lectures. The second question was on the subject matter of their preaching. Ignatius gently corrected the subprior in saying that they did not preach, that is, they did not give formal discourses but rather spoke familiarly with those who came to listen. Theirs was more of a chat than a sermon. And as for the content, they spoke about virtue and sin. The subprior then came to the heart of his interrogation: If Ignatius was instructing others about virtue and sin and since he was not educated in that area, as he himself acknowledged, then the knowledge he had must

[2] See *OC* 129 n. 1; *GV* 296. On Ignatius' stay at the Dominican monastery, see V. Beltrán de Heredia, "Estancia de San Ignacio de Loyola en San Esteban de Salamanca", *La Ciencia Tomista* 70 (1956): 507–28.

talk about virtue and vice? No one can speak of these except in either of two ways: either because of having been educated, or by the Holy Spirit. Since you have had no education, then it is by the Holy Spirit." The pilgrim was now on his guard, for this way of arguing did not seem good to him.

have come to him by direct illumination of the Holy Spirit. Ignatius immediately saw the corner into which the subprior was trying to force him. If he said his knowledge came from the Holy Spirit, he would be admitting that he was an *alumbrado*, and since these "enlightened ones" had been condemned by the Inquisition in Toledo on September 23, 1525,[3] he would be condemning himself. Though not trained in the schools, Ignatius had learned much from his various confessors, from the spiritual people with whom he spoke, from his reading, as well as from his own personal ordeal with scruples.

Ignatius wisely declined to continue the conversation, but the subprior insisted, desirous of discovering whether Ignatius held opinions similar to those of Desiderius Erasmus,[4] or to those of the Lutherans, whose teaching had recently penetrated Spain. The friars at San Esteban were especially interested in Erasmus at this time because a conference of theologians was then meeting in Valladolid, having been convened by the Inquisitor General, Alonso Manrique, Archbishop of Seville.[5] The purpose of that conference was to discuss twenty-one propositions taken from Erasmus' works and to judge whether they were consonant with Catholic teaching or whether they were heretical. Because of this "Erasmus fever" in the air, the subprior pressed hard on Ignatius to reveal himself.

---

[3] See *GV* 279.

[4] Erasmus of Rotterdam (1446–1536) was the most celebrated humanist of his day. His adversaries claimed that he attacked the basic institutions of the Church and had prepared the way for Luther.

[5] The conference began on June 27 and ended on August 13, 1527. At this conference the Dominicans and Franciscans manifested themselves as Erasmus' most bitter opponents. Though twenty-one propositions were excerpted from Erasmus' writings, the theologians at the conference discussed only two, and since the participants were unable to come to any agreement, the Grand Inquisitor suspended the conference without passing any judgment on Erasmus.

After a bit of silence he said there was no further need to discuss these matters. The friar pressed on: "With so many errors now deceiving the world, as those of Erasmus and of many others, you are unwilling to explain what you mean?"

66. The pilgrim replied: "Father, I will say nothing more than what I have said, except in the presence of my superiors who can oblige me to do so." Before this the friar had asked why Calixto came dressed as he did. He wore a short coat with a large hat on his head, a staff in his hand, and boots halfway up his legs. Since he was very tall, all this made him look quite ridiculous. The pilgrim told him the story of how they had been imprisoned in Alcalá and that they had been ordered to wear the clothes that students wore, and since it was very hot his companion had given his long student's gown to a poor cleric. Here the friar, making it clear that this did not please him, mumbled between his teeth, "Charity begins at home."

But returning to the story, the subprior, not being able to get another word out of the pilgrim except that one, said:

66–67. Since the subprior was not his ecclesiastical superior, Ignatius refused to continue the discussion. But now that the subprior's suspicions had been aroused, he asked Ignatius and Calixto to remain at the monastery. Their stay there lasted three days, during which time the subprior took Ignatius' case to the diocesan court judges to initiate proceedings against him, but never was Ignatius informed that the friars were bringing him to trial. At the end of the three days, Ignatius and Calixto were taken to a prison, and their cell, though not a dungeon and not with common criminals, was musty, filthy, and rodent infested.[6] The chain binding their legs was about a yard long, and since they were without mats for sleeping and had rodents wandering freely about, it is no wonder that their first night was sleepless.

---

[6] Polanco says that the room was dark and "had a great number of different kinds of animals" (*FN* 1:175–76).

"Remain here; we will easily get you to tell all." All the friars then departed in some haste. First the pilgrim asked if they wanted them to wait in that chapel or anywhere else they might want them to wait. The subprior answered that they were to remain in the chapel. The friars then locked all the doors and went, it seems, to discuss the matter with judges. The two of them stayed at the monastery for three days, eating in the refectory with the monks, without anything being said to them about a trial. Their room was almost always full of friars who came to see them, and the pilgrim always spoke about the things he usually talked about. As a consequence a division arose among the monks, for many showed that their sympathy was with them.

Bachelor Frías,[7] called by the title bachelor to distinguish him from another judge with the same name, questioned both prisoners. On learning where their companions Arteaga and Cáceres were lodging, Frías sent prison attendants to arrest them as well, but these two were placed in an underground cell. Only Juanico remained free, perhaps because of his youth. Ignatius mentions, without giving any time reference, that Juanico became a friar; other sources indicate that he entered the Franciscans.[8] With this preliminary interrogation over, Frías left the prison, taking with him Ignatius' copy of the Exercises. There is no way of knowing how developed the Exercises were at this time—were they already in an early-draft stage, or were they still a collection of notes that would eventually become what we now know as the Spiritual Exercises?

---

[7] At one time this Frías was thought to be Martín de Frías (*FN* 1:456 n. 5), but now he is thought to be Sancho (González) de Frías, canon of Salamanca, who later became vicar general to Francisco de Bobadilla, Bishop of Salamanca. See B. Hernández Montés, "Identidad de los personajes que juzgaron a San Ignacio en Salamanca: Problemas historicos suscitados por las primeras fuentes", *Archivum Historicum Societatis Iesu* 52 (1983): 3–50.

[8] See *FN* 1:458 n. 6.

67. At the end of three days a notary came and led them to prison. They were not put underground with the criminals, but in an upper room, which, because it was old and unused, contained a lot of rubbish. They were bound together by one and the same chain, each by his foot; the chain was about ten to thirteen palms long, and every time one wanted to do something, the other had to go with him. All that night they remained awake. The following day, when the news spread in the city that they were in prison, their friends sent them mats for sleeping and an abundant supply of whatever else they needed. Many kept on coming to see them, and the pilgrim continued in his practice of speaking about God, and so forth.

Bachelor Frías came to question them individually, and the pilgrim gave him all his notes, which were the Exercises, for examination. Asked if they had companions, they said they did and told where they were. Following the bachelor's order, they immediately went there and brought Cáceres and Arteaga to the prison, but left behind Juanico, who later became a friar. They did not place them in the upper room with the other two, but below, where the ordinary prisoners were kept. Here also he did not want to have any lawyer or attorney.

68. Several days later he was summoned before four judges: the Doctors were Sanctisidoro, Paravinhas, and Frías, and the fourth was Bachelor Frías, all of whom had already seen the Exercises. They now questioned him about many things, not only about the Exercises, but in theology, for example, on

68. After the four judges appointed to hear the case had read through the Exercises, they called Ignatius to appear before them. Three were doctors of law and the fourth was Bachelor Frías. Of the doctors whose names Ignatius records, scholars agree that the Sanctisidoro may have been

the Trinity and the Blessed Sacrament, and how he understood these articles of faith. He first gave an introduction,
but being ordered by the judges, he spoke in such a way that
they had no reason whatever to censure him. Bachelor Frías,
who always pressed him more than the others, also asked a
question in canon law. Being obliged to answer every question, he always prefaced his remarks saying that he did not
know what the learned doctors held on these points. Then
they ordered him to explain the First Commandment as he
usually explained it. This he started to do, and did it in so
great detail, saying so many things about the First Commandment that they no longer had any desire to ask anything more of him. Previously, when they were discussing

Fernando Rodríguez de San Isidoro and that Frías was probably Francisco
de Frías.[9] Neither the name Paravinhas nor one similar to it appears in the
Salamanca diocesan records. A copyist may have made an unwitting or-
thographic change in the name.[10] Ignatius successfully answered all the
questions asked him, whether on the Trinity or the Eucharist, and so
thorough was his explanation of the First Commandment that the judges
did not want to sit through similar lengthy expositions for the other nine.
On one topic, however, the judges showed great tenacity. In the Exercises,
in the part entitled "General Examen of Conscience", Ignatius speaks of
sins of thought and gives guidelines on how to determine whether these
thoughts are mortally or venially sinful. What perplexed the learned judges
was that someone as theologically uneducated as Ignatius should be capable of determining whether a thought is a mortal or a venial sin. Unable
to condemn any portion of Ignatius' explanation, the judges brought the
interrogation to a close.

---

[9] See *OC* 130 n. 7; *FN* 1:458 n. 7. B. Hernández, in his above-cited articles, gives the former's name as Hernán Rodríguez de San Isidro.

[10] So maintains *FN* 1:458 n. 6 and *GV* 298 n. 56. On the other hand, B.
Hernández suggests, in his article, that the judge's name was Alonso Gómez de
Paradinas, who was vicar general of the Salamanca diocese at the time that
Ignatius was in the city.

the Exercises, they showed great insistence on a single point, which is at the beginning of the Exercises: When is a thought a venial sin, and when is it a mortal sin? Their problem was that he, though uneducated, was determining that question. He responded: "Decide whether what I say is true or not; if is not true, condemn it." In the end they left without condemning anything.

69. Among the many who came to see him in prison was Don Francisco de Mendoza, who is now Cardinal of Burgos, and on that occasion he came with Bachelor Frías. Speaking as a friend would, he asked how he was getting along in prison and whether being there weighed heavily upon him. He replied: "As my answer I will give the same that I today gave a lady who, when seeing me imprisoned, spoke words of compassion. I told her: 'By this you show that you do not desire to be taken prisoner for the love of God. Does imprisonment appear to be so great an evil to you? Then I will tell you that there are not enough fetters and chains in Salamanca that I would not desire more for the love of God.'"

69. The one visitor that Ignatius mentions by name was Don Francisco de Mendoza.[11] At the time of his visit he was only nineteen and was teaching Greek at the University of Salamanca. Ignatius' answer to him should not be read as if he rejected Mendoza's expression of compassion but as Ignatius seeing his days of confinement as days of praise to God and that he was willing to bear even greater suffering for the love of God.

When there was a jailbreak among the inmates in the dungeon area and Arteaga and Cáceres refused to escape with the others, the prison officials were greatly moved by their innate goodness and honesty. In recognition of Arteaga's and Cáceres' integrity, Ignatius and his companions were moved to a nearby residence, where they were kept under house arrest.

---

[11] Mendoza became a cardinal in 1545 and was later transferred to the see of Burgos in 1550. He died in 1566.

At this time it happened that all the prisoners made their escape, but the two companions who were with them did not flee. When they were found the next morning, all alone with doors wide open, everyone was deeply edified, and this caused much talk in the city. Because of this they put all of them in a nearby mansion as their prison.

70. After twenty-two days of imprisonment they were summoned to hear their sentence. No error was discovered either in their life-style or in their teaching; therefore they could continue as they had been doing, teaching doctrine and speaking about the things of God, as long as they did not determine "this is a mortal sin" or "this is a venial sin", until they had completed four years of study. When the sentence was read, the judges manifested great kindness, since they wanted them to agree to the sentence. The pilgrim said that he would fulfill all that the sentence ordered, but that he did not agree with it, for though not condemning him on any single point, they were forcing his mouth closed so as to keep him from helping others in the way that he could. Though Doctor Frías strongly urged them to agree, and gave signs that he was sympathetic, the pilgrim said nothing else except that as long as he remained within the jurisdiction of Salamanca, he would do as had been ordered.

70. As in his previous encounters with ecclesiastical courts, no error was found in Ignatius' teaching. Unlike the Alcalá sentence, Ignatius and his companions were permitted to continue their apostolate, but with the single restriction of not determining, until they had completed four years of formal theological training, whether a thought is mortally or venially sinful.

Ignatius made known his willingness to obey the sentence, but he did mention that he did not agree with it. Since he was accused of no error whatever and since it was imperative in Ignatius' eyes to teach the faithful how to distinguish between mortal and venial sins in order to avoid

Then and there they were released from prison, and he began to commend the matter to God and to think of what he should do. He found great difficulty in staying in Salamanca because this prohibition on determining which are mortal and which are venial sins closed the door on his helping souls.

71. Thus he decided on going to Paris to study. In Barcelona, when the pilgrim was deliberating whether he should study and for how many years, his main concern was whether, after his studies, he should enter religion or continue going about the world. With the thought of entering religion, he also thought of entering a congregation that was lax and

---

scruples and to make their confessions more fruitful, he interpreted this sentence as forcibly silencing him in the very areas where he could best help others. The four companions, now released from prison, had to think of their future.

71–72. A couple of years before, when Ignatius was in Barcelona, he had wondered whether he should give himself to studies—he was in his thirties—and whether after studies he should enter a religious order or continue as he was in the world. Because of the desire he then had of doing great penances, the thought of entering a lax congregation seemed to fit in with his plans. Perhaps God, taking into account his penitential life, would inspire such a congregation to reform. For himself, he was certain that he was capable of enduring all the personal affronts that others could heap upon him. But after his days in Barcelona he was convinced that he was called by God to help others, and during his incarceration in Salamanca this desire to help others was always foremost in his thoughts. If he were now to join a religious order, it would have been the Conventual Franciscans, because of their work among the faithful, rather than the more cloistered Observants.[12] But he first had to begin his studies if he wanted to be of help to others, and so Ignatius decided on going to the University of Paris. He told his companions that he would go ahead and would find the money for them to follow him.

---

[12] See *FN* 2:137–38.

unreformed so that he could suffer more in it. He thought that God would perhaps help it, for God granted him a deep assurance that he could successfully endure all the insults and hurts that they might inflict upon him.

During the period of his imprisonment in Salamanca he was not without the same desire to help souls, and with that as his goal he decided to study and to win over like-minded individuals and keep those he had. Once he had decided on going to Paris, he arranged with the other companions to wait where they were while he went to see if he could find the means by which they could also study.

72. Many prominent individuals urgently begged him not to leave, but they could never convince him. Fifteen or twenty days after leaving prison, he set out by himself, carrying some books on a donkey. When he came to Barcelona, all who knew him tried to dissuade him from going to France because of the violent battles going on there, and they narrated many specific incidents, even telling him that they skewered Spaniards on spits. But never did he have any fear.

Hearing of Ignatius' desire to leave Salamanca, his friends tried to talk him out of his plans, but two or three weeks after his release from prison he set out, in mid-September, with a donkey carrying his books. The total time he spent in Salamanca was about two months, and never did he get to enter Archbishop Fonseca's college for poor students. During his time in Salamanca someone gave him books that would be of use to him in his studies, and someone else supplied him with a donkey to make the trip easier. When Ignatius came to Barcelona his friends there also tried to talk him out of traveling to France, going to such extremes as to narrate horror stories of what the French were supposed to be doing to Spaniards when apprehended. With complete confidence in God, Ignatius resolutely set his face toward Paris and looked to the future.

Chapter 8

Paris: University Studies
and First Companions

(February 2, 1528–April 1535)

73. Alone and on foot he set out for Paris and arrived
there in the month of February, more or less. I think it was
in the year 1528 or 1527. He found lodging in a house with
several Spaniards and began studying the humanities at Montaigu. The reason why he did this was because they had made
him advance through his studies with such great haste that
he found that he was without a good foundation. He went

73. After a good month's walk of almost seven hundred miles, and in
the cold of winter, Ignatius finally arrived in the City of Light, his home
for the next six years. He left no record of the cities he visited or of any
incident along the way. Because of the time of year his route to Paris must
have been the most direct,[1] bringing him there on February 2, 1528.[2] He
passed through Porte Saint-Jacques, and using the few French words he

---

[1] *PY* 190 suggests that Ignatius' route to Paris may have been as follows:
Barcelona, Perpignan, Narbonne, Carcassonne, Toulouse, Cahors, Limoges,
Bourges, Orléans, and finally Paris.

[2] Writing to Inés Pascual on March 3, 1528, Ignatius says: "Favored by the
weather and in perfect health, by the grace and goodness of God our Lord, I
arrived in this city of Paris, where I shall continue my studies until it please the
Lord to ordain otherwise, on the second day of February" (*LW* 180).

to class with young lads and made progress according to the prescribed curriculum of Paris.

As soon as he arrived in Paris a shopkeeper gave him twenty-five *escudos* on a draft from Barcelona, and these he gave to one of the Spaniards where he was staying for safe-keeping, but the Spaniard squandered them in a very short time and had no way of repaying him. When Lent was over, the pilgrim had no money because of what he had spent as well as for the above-mentioned reason, and thus he was

had learned on the way, he found where the Spaniards made their home in that great city. As he was leaving Barcelona his friends had forced upon him a draft of twenty-five *escudos*, redeemable in Paris; this was meant to supply him with the funds he would need to get settled and then to begin his studies. After redeeming the draft, he gave the money to a compatriot for safekeeping. Because he himself was honest, he thought everyone else was honest.

Classes were in session, and Ignatius registered at Collège de Montaigu but discovered, after an entrance exam, that his background was still in-sufficient for advanced work. Thus he decided to repeat these courses, attending classes with boys in their early teens and even younger. When he successfully passed one stage, he advanced to another, following the established program of studies then in force in Paris. Montaigu[3] was one of the more than fifty colleges making up the University of Paris and one of the schools frequented by Spanish and Portuguese students. When Eas-ter came—April 12 that year—he discovered that his trust in his fellow Spaniard had been misplaced, for he now found himself without a cent. He had no other alternative but to beg his bread, and since he was no longer able to pay for his room, he began searching for a place that would accept him in as a nonpaying guest.

---

[3] The college had been founded in the fourteenth century and was named after Gilles Aycelin de Montaigu, Archbishop of Rouen. It was located on Paris' left bank, and among its more famous students were Erasmus, Rabelais, and Calvin, who had left the college just a few days before Ignatius arrived. The college building no longer stands; in its place is the Bibliothèque Sainte-Geneviève, near the Pantheon.

forced to go begging and even had to leave the house where he was staying.

74. He was accepted at the Hospital Saint-Jacques, beyond the church of the Innocents. This was especially inconvenient for his classes since the hospital was a good distance from the Collège de Montaigu, and he had to return home before the ringing of the *Ave Maria* in order to find the door open, and he had to leave at daylight. As a result he could not conveniently attend his lectures. Another drawback was the fact that he had to beg alms in order to support himself.

About five years had passed since he had had any stomach pain, and so he began to fast and practice greater penances. Living for some time in this way, at the hospital and by begging, and seeing that he was making little progress in his studies, he started to think about what he should do. He knew that there were some who served several of the regents in the college and had time for their studies, so he decided to look for someone to hire him.

74–75. Ignatius found a room at the Hospital Saint-Jacques,[4] a hospice for pilgrims on their way to Santiago de Compostela. Living at the hospital proved a great disadvantage to him. Though it was more than a mile walk to the Montaigu, it was not the walking that distressed the lame Ignatius but the fact that the horarium at the hospital conflicted with that of the college. The hospital opened its doors only when the sun rose and closed them early with the sound of the evening Angelus. Ignatius' first class, on the other hand, was at 5 a.m. and his last at 6 p.m.,[5] which meant missing both classes. Many such absences, together with the time spent in begging, had their effect on his classwork. Since his chief purpose for being in Paris was to study, he judged that he could not long continue

---

[4] The hospital, located on the right bank, was founded in 1323. Neither the hospital nor the church of the Holy Innocents remains today. The site of the former hospital is today's 133 rue Saint-Denis. See *GV* 310 n. 10.

[5] For the schedule of classes at Montaigu, see *GV* 309 n. 9.

75. He kept mulling over this idea and found consolation in it because he imagined that his master would be Christ, and to one student he gave the name Saint Peter and to another Saint John, and so on with each of the apostles. "When the master gives me an order I will think that it is Christ commanding me, and when someone else gives me an order I will think that it is Saint Peter commanding me." He tried his hardest to find an employer, and on one occasion he spoke to Bachelor Castro, and on another to a Carthusian friar, who was acquainted with many of the masters, and to others, too, but they were never able to find a job for him.

76. Not finding any solution, he was eventually told by a Spanish friar that it would be better for him to go each year

living at the hospital but would have to seek another arrangement. It might be possible, he thought, to secure a position as servant to one of the younger professors in one of the colleges. Such a position would give him his room and board and supply him with some funds to pay for his education, and it would also allow him the time he needed for his studies. He took this idea to Juan Castro,[6] who had recently received his bachelor's degree, asking him if he knew of anyone who could employ him, but neither Castro nor a Carthusian monk nor any of the others whom he had asked was able to do anything for him.

76. Ignatius made his first begging tour to Flanders during Lent 1529. Flanders was an ideal place for such a tour, not only because it was part of the Spanish empire, but because its two centers of international

---

[6] Juan Castro was born in Burgos, Spain, in 1485. When Ignatius got to know him, he was teaching at the Sorbonne and working toward his doctorate in theology, which he received in 1532. He returned to Spain and in 1535 entered the Charterhouse of Val de Cristo near Segorbe, and Ignatius visited him there, as he mentions in no. 90. In 1542 Castro became prior of the Charterhouse of Porta Coeli in Valencia and died there in 1556. Val de Cristo remained a monastery until 1834, when it was suppressed by the government; the buildings are now in ruins. Porta Coeli still exists as a monastery. See *OC* 134 n. 7, and *FX* 137 n. 240.

to Flanders, giving up two months or less, and to return with enough funds to study for an entire year. After he had commended this idea to God, it seemed good to him, and following that advice each year he brought back from Flanders enough so that he could continue in some way. Once he even went to England and brought back more alms than he usually did in other years.

77. Upon his return from Flanders he began with greater earnestness than before to hold spiritual conversations and

commerce, Bruges and Antwerp, had a large number of wealthy Spanish merchants. It was to these that Ignatius went. On his first visit to Bruges, Ignatius met and dined with the celebrated Spanish humanist Juan Luis Vives,[7] who once had been private secretary to the English Queen Catherine of Aragon. He was relieved of that position when he refused to go along with Henry VIII's desire to divorce her. Ignatius' trip to Flanders was a success, and since his life-style was simple and spartan, what he collected was sufficient to support him for a full year and to help other poor students as well. His second and third trips there were during the months of August and September 1530 and 1531. He again visited his merchant friends, but rather than having him return to Flanders each year, many of them agreed to send their contributions in the future directly to him in Paris. After the visit of 1531, perhaps encouraged to do so by Vives, Ignatius went over to London,[8] and from the Spanish merchants in the English capital he collected more funds than he usually collected after weeks in Flanders.

77–78. Since his visit to Flanders had proven worthwhile, Ignatius left the inconveniently located Hospital Saint-Jacques and found a room some-

---

[7] Juan Luis Vives was born in Valencia, Spain, in 1492. He studied in Paris and in 1519 became professor of humanities at Louvain and was friendly with Erasmus. He taught at Corpus Christi College, Oxford, and received a Doctor of Laws from that same institution. He became court counselor and education advisor to Henry VIII. He died in Bruges in 1540. For Ignatius' dinner with him, see *FN* 2:557 or *GV* 313–16.

[8] Willem A. M. Peters suggests that Ignatius, while in England, stayed at Syon Monastery. See his "Richard Whitford and St. Ignatius' Visit to England", *Archivum Historicum Societatis Iesu* 25 (1956): 328–50.

was giving the Exercises, almost simultaneously, to three individuals, that is, to Peralta, to Bachelor Castro, who was at the Sorbonne, and to Amador, a Basque who was at Sainte-Barbe. These men underwent great changes, and they promptly gave all that they had to the poor, even their books, and took up begging alms in Paris. They went to live in the Hospital Saint-Jacques, where the pilgrim had once stayed and whence he had left for the reasons given above. This caused a great tumult in the university, for the first two were distinguished and famous personages. Without wasting any time the Spanish students entered into heated argument with the two masters, but unable to get them to return to the university, either by persuasion or reason, a large group of the students, one day, with arms in their hands, went and hauled their masters from the hospital.

where in the university district itself and began giving the Exercises to three of his acquaintances. Juan Castro[9] was then teaching at the Sorbonne, Pedro de Peralta[10] was living at Montaigu and completing his master's degree, and Amador de Elduayen,[11] a fellow Guipúzcoan, was a student at Collège de Sainte-Barbe, located directly across from Montaigu. As a result of the meditations that Ignatius had given these young men, the three had decided to relinquish their academic careers, give away whatever belongings they possessed, and enter upon a life of poverty. They lived in the hospital where Ignatius had lived and begged their food in the Paris streets. Their decision seems to have come about while Ignatius was

---

[9] See n. 6 above.

[10] Pedro de Peralta came from the diocese of Toledo and received his master's degree in 1529. After attempting to make a pilgrimage to the Holy Land, he returned to Toledo and became a canon at the cathedral and a famous preacher. He always retained affection for Ignatius and the Society. See OC 135 n. 9.

[11] Not much is known about Amador de Elduayen except that he came from Guipúzcoa and had matriculated at the university in 1526. See OC 135 n. 9; FX 138 n. 242.

78. Upon bringing the masters back to the university, they all agreed on the following: after the masters had completed their courses they could then proceed with their plans. Bachelor Castro later went to Spain, was a preacher in Burgos for a time, and then became a Carthusian friar near Segorbe. Peralta set out on foot as a pilgrim for Jerusalem. He was detained in Italy by a captain, a relative of his, who saw to it that he was brought before the pope and that he was commanded to return to Spain. These things happened, not immediately, but some years later.

In Paris a slander campaign began against the pilgrim, especially among the Spaniards. Our Master de Gouvea said that he [the pilgrim] had turned Amador, who was a mem-

---

absent from Paris on a mission of charity to Rouen (see no. 79). Though Castro and Peralta had given up their teaching positions, the students would not go along with their desire. They considered this change in them a temporary derangement. When they were unable to bring their masters back to the university by peaceable means, the students resorted to force and physically dragged them back and would not set them free until both had agreed to complete the courses they had begun.

Since Castro and Peralta had become attached to Ignatius, the Spanish students held Ignatius responsible for their madness. Diogo de Gouvea,[12] principal at Sainte-Barbe, was likewise angered with Ignatius, since his student, Amador, had fallen under the latter's influence. Gouvea's wrath reached such a peak that he swore that if Ignatius were ever to visit Sainte-Barbe, he would have him undergo the shameful punishment of a public flogging. Ignatius refers to him as "our master", the usual title the students gave to their professors who had received an advanced degree. Gouvea's anger was short-lived, for within weeks of this threat Ignatius moved from Montaigu to Sainte-Barbe.

In time both Castro and Peralta returned to Spain, and at the time when Ignatius was narrating these events, Castro was prior of the Charter-

---

[12] Diogo de Gouvea (c. 1471–1557), a Portuguese, governed Collège de Sainte-Barbe from 1520 to 1548. See OC 136 n. 10.

ber of his college, into a madman and that he [de Gouvea] was determined, so he said, that the first time he [the pilgrim] set foot in Sainte-Barbe, he would give him a public whipping in the hall for being a seducer of students.

79. The Spaniard with whom he had stayed in the beginning and who had squandered his money without repaying it left for Spain by way of Rouen. While waiting for passage in Rouen, he fell ill. Learning from a letter of his that he was quite sick, the pilgrim had the desire to go visit and assist him. At the same time he thought that through such a meeting he could win him over, so that he would leave the world and devote himself totally to the service of God.

In order to accomplish his purpose, he intended to cover twenty-eight leagues from Paris to Rouen by walking barefoot and without eating or drinking. While praying over this proposal he found that he became filled with fright, and, finally, he went to the church of Saint Dominic and there

---

house of Porta Coeli in Valencia and Peralta was a famous preacher in Toledo's cathedral.

79. After he had given the Exercises to Castro, Peralta, and Amador, Ignatius received a letter from the Spaniard who had previously squandered his money, informing him that he was in Rouen on his way to Spain but had fallen ill. The writer undoubtedly realized that his letter would touch Ignatius and that he would come to him without being asked. Setting aside the fact that the man had once cheated him, Ignatius made up his mind to help him in any way he could. He also thought he might be able to convert the man, and so Ignatius decided to make the journey into a penance. Not only would he walk that distance barefoot, but he would do it without food or drink. Such a harsh penance would cause fear in anyone, but Ignatius would not permit it to sway his thinking, and so he went to the nearby Dominican church on rue Saint-Jacques to ask God to grant him the strength to carry out what he had determined to do. He set out for Rouen sometime in September, and though he started his journey filled with fear, it finally left him after he had passed Argenteuil, which

determined to go ahead with his plans, for his great fear that he was tempting God had now left him.

The following day, the morning of his departure, he woke up very early, and as he was about to get dressed so great a dread took hold of him that it was almost as if he were unable to dress himself. Still feeling this aversion, he left the house and the city before full daylight. That fear stayed with him and lasted until Argenteuil, which is a fortified town three leagues from Paris on the road to Rouen and where our Lord's robe is said to be. He passed by that fortress, still suffering his spiritual anguish, but as he climbed a hill that anguish began to disappear. Great consolation and spiritual strength took its place and with so much joy that he began to shout over the fields and speak aloud to God, and so forth. He spent that night with a poor beggar in a hospital, having walked fourteen leagues that day. The following night he spent in a barn, and on the third day he reached Rouen—all this time eating and drinking nothing, and barefoot just as he had planned. In Rouen he consoled the sick man and

was only six miles from Paris and was famous in the Middle Ages for possessing one of Christ's robes.[13] Walking more than half that distance on the first day—the remainder of the trip was more difficult because of his hunger and thirst—Ignatius covered the seventy-six miles in three days. He found the sick Spaniard and comforted him not only with words, but cared for him, and when a ship was about to sail for Spain he assisted him aboard and probably helped defray the man's passage. In return for all this Ignatius only asked him to deliver letters to his three friends in Salamanca. The fact that there was no letter for Juanico probably indicates that somewhere between Ignatius' departure from Salamanca (September 1527) and the present (September 1529), Juanico had become a Franciscan.

---

[13] For more on this seamless robe of Christ, see Joan Carroll Cruz, *Relics* (Huntington, Ind.: Our Sunday Visitor, 1984), 23–27.

helped him board a ship going to Spain and gave him letters addressed to his companions in Salamanca, namely to Calixto, Cáceres, and Arteaga.

80. To avoid saying anything more about these companions, this is what happened to them.

The pilgrim frequently wrote to them from Paris, as they had agreed, about the slight chance there was of bringing

---

80. Ignatius interrupts the natural flow of his narrative to tell us what eventually happened to his three companions. He kept in touch with them, but because he had barely enough resources to sustain himself, he could not, at that time, ask the three to come to Paris. In the case of Calixto there was some hope. Calixto may have been of Portuguese stock, since Ignatius asked Doña Leonor Mascarenhas[14] to write to the Portuguese king requesting for him one of the scholarships that the king had founded at Sainte-Barbe. It is unknown whether a scholarship was offered to Calixto or not; in any case, he did not go to Paris. In 1531 he went to "the emperor's India", the common name then for Mexico.[15] When he returned after his second visit, he came back a rich man and settled down in Salamanca.

As for Cáceres, Ignatius' brief statement may indicate his disappointment in him. Arteaga seems to have done well for himself. He received not only worldly honors but likewise ecclesiastical honors, for he was appointed Bishop of Chiapas in Mexico. When he arrived in Veracruz he was already sick but continued on to Mexico City, where the unfortunate accident happened.[16]

---

[14] Doña Leonor Mascarenhas (1503–1584) was a noble Portuguese who had come to Spain with Infanta Isabella when the latter married Charles V in 1526. She remained as a lady-in-waiting and served as governess to the young Philip II. Ignatius may have met her when he went to visit Archbishop Fonseca in Valladolid in 1527. See OC 138 n. 15. For further details of her life, see LW 417–33.

[15] At the time of Calixto's first visit to Mexico he was only twenty-four or twenty-five years old. The "spiritually inclined lady" that Ignatius mentions was Catalina Hernández, a native of Salamanca. See OC 140 n. 16.

[16] The original text identifies the poison as *acqua di solimano* (Spanish *aqua de solimán*). *Solimán* means "corrosive sublimate", but its chemical make-up is mercuric chloride.

them to Paris to study. But he wrote a letter to Doña Leonor
Mascarenhas, asking her to assist Calixto by writing a letter
to the court of the King of Portugal so that he could be
given one of the scholarships that the king had established in
Paris. Doña Leonor gave the letter to Calixto, with a mule
for the journey and money for expenses. Calixto went to
the Portuguese king's court, but in the end he did not come
to Paris. When he returned to Spain he went to "the emperor's India" with a certain spiritually inclined lady. He later
returned to Spain and again went to the same India and then
came back to Spain a wealthy man, astonishing all who had
previously known him in Salamanca.

Cáceres returned to Segovia, his birthplace, and began to live
in such a way that he seems to have forgotten his earlier resolves.

Arteaga had been raised to a knighthood. Later, when
the Society was established in Rome, he was given a bish-
opric in India, and he wrote to the pilgrim asking that it
be given to someone in the Society, but the pilgrim responded negatively to it. He was made a bishop and went
to India and died there in a most strange manner: during
his illness, there were two bottles of water for his refresh-
ment; one had the water that the physician had prescribed
for him, the other contained water with a corrosive sublimate, a poison, and this latter was given to him by mis-
take, and it killed him.

81. The pilgrim returned to Paris from Rouen and learned
that widespread rumors had been broadcast against him because of what had happened to Castro and Peralta and that
the inquisitor had asked about him. Not wanting to wait any

---

81. Ignatius returned to Paris sometime in the latter part of September,
when the Castro-Peralta tumult had subsided. But during his absence his

longer, he went to the inquisitor, telling him that he had heard that he had been looking for him and that he was ready for whatever he might wish. (The inquisitor was our Master Ory, a friar of Saint Dominic.) He [the pilgrim] asked him to hurry the matter along because he intended to begin his courses in the liberal arts on the feast of Saint Remy and he would first like to have this over so that he could better attend to his studies. The inquisitor never again called him, but only told him that it was true that they had spoken about his activities, and so on.

82. Shortly after this came the feast of Saint Remy, which is the beginning of October, and he sat in on courses in the liberal arts under a teacher whose name was Master Juan Peña.

name had been brought before the Inquisition,[17] and inquiries had been made about him. Immediately after his return he went directly to the Dominican monastery where Master Ory[18] resided, presented himself, and requested that the investigation not be postponed since classes were soon to begin. The fact that Master Ory never again summoned Ignatius signifies that the Castro-Peralta affair had completely abated.

82. Toward the end of September 1529, Ignatius matriculated at Collège de Sainte-Barbe[19] and was to begin his study of philosophy on October 1, the feast of Saint Remy. He was assigned to live with three others:

---

[17] It has been suggested that it was Dr. Pedro Ortiz (1501–1548) who brought the accusation against Ignatius before the Inquisition. He lived at Montaigu and had been Peralta's patron. In 1529 Ortiz went to Salamanca to teach Scripture, and from the end of 1530 he represented Charles V in Rome in regard to Henry VIII's request for a divorce. In Rome Ortiz and Ignatius became close friends and Ignatius took him through the Exercises, as he mentions in no. 98. See *FX* 139 n. 245.

[18] Matthieu Ory, O.P., was a Breton who received his doctorate in 1526 and then taught theology in the Dominican monastery of Saint-Jacques. He became prior of the monastery in 1535 and died in 1557. See *FX* 249 n. 16.

[19] The college was founded in 1460 and had Saint Barbara as its patron. Of the medieval collegiate structures in Paris, it is one of the few still standing. Its entrance today is 4 rue Valette, near the Pantheon.

He began his courses intending to keep those companions who had determined to serve the Lord, and not go about looking to add others, so that he could comfortably give himself to his studies.

Master Juan Peña,[20] who was then teaching philosophy at Sainte-Barbe and was to be Ignatius' teacher, and two students, Pierre Favre,[21] a Savoyard, and Francis Xavier,[22] a Navarrese. Favre and Xavier had been in Paris since 1525. They were fifteen years younger than Ignatius and had already attained their bachelor's degrees. Ignatius' firm intention was to spend his time on his studies, while keeping in contact with the friends he had made. He knew he would not have the leisure to search out new companions.

As soon as he settled into the rhythm of his lectures, Ignatius was afflicted by the same problem he had experienced in Barcelona, of spiritual thoughts invading his mind and bringing him distraction. Since he had once had this temptation and had overcome it, he surmised that the

---

[20] Juan Peña came from the diocese of Sigüenza, Spain. He received his master's degree in 1525 and taught philosophy at Sainte-Barbe while he continued his studies in medicine. See *OC* 141 n. 21.

[21] Pierre Favre was born in Villaret, Savoy, France, on April 13, 1506, went to Paris in 1525, and received his licentiate degree in March 1530. He was ordained to the priesthood on May 30, 1534, and celebrated his first Mass on July 22, 1534. As a Jesuit he traveled widely, making the Society known in Italy, Germany, and Spain. He returned to Rome and died there on August 1, 1546. On September 5, 1872, Pope Pius IX, acknowledging the cult that had been paid to Favre in his native Savoy, confirmed it by apostolic decree and declared that Favre was among the blessed in heaven. His feast day is celebrated on August 2.

[22] Francisco de Jassu y Javier was born in Navarre, Spain, on April 7, 1506. He went to Paris in 1525, received his licentiate degree in 1530, and began teaching philosophy at Collège de Dormans-Beauvais. Francis arrived in Rome in 1538 and in 1540 was appointed to the Society's mission in India. He left Portugal in April 1541 and arrived in Goa in May 1542. As a missionary, Xavier labored in India, Malaya, and Japan, and he was waiting to enter China when he died on December 3, 1552. Xavier was declared blessed by Pope Paul V on October 25, 1619, and canonized by Pope Gregory XV on March 12, 1622. His feast is celebrated on December 3.

As he began to attend the lectures in his course, the same temptations began to disturb him as those that had come when he was studying grammar in Barcelona. Whenever he was at a lecture, he was unable to remain attentive because of the many spiritual thoughts that came to him. Realizing that he was, in this way, gaining little profit from the lectures, he went to his teacher and promised never to be absent but to

remedy used then would also work now. So he went to Master Peña to explain why he had not been doing well, and he promised to be faithful in attending class and in studying. To help him catch up with the others, Master Peña asked Favre to help Ignatius by tutoring him.

During his years at Sainte-Barbe Ignatius gained six additional companions, though he did not go in search of them. His first disciples were his roommates, Favre and Xavier. The next to join him was Simão Rodrigues,[23] a Portuguese, who had been at Sainte-Barbe since 1527 but who did not become friendly with Ignatius until October 1532. The next two were Spaniards, Diego Laínez[24] and Alfonso Salmerón.[25] Both had

---

[23] Simão Rodrigues was born of noble parents in 1510 in the village of Vouzella in the diocese of Viseu in northern Portugal. He was first educated in Lisbon, then came to Paris in 1527 and studied at Collège de Sainte-Barbe. In his career as a Jesuit he was superior (1540–1546) and provincial (1546–1552) of the Portuguese province. In 1553 he was called to Italy, where he remained until 1564, when he went to Spain. In 1573 he returned to Portugal and died there in 1579.

[24] Diego Laínez was born in 1512 in Almazán, Spain. He attended the University of Alcalá, arriving there after Ignatius had left for Salamanca. He earned his master's degree at Alcalá in 1532 and then began his study of theology. He went to Paris in 1533 to meet Ignatius. Later in life Laínez served as papal theologian at the Council of Trent (1546, 1551, and 1562). He was named provincial of Italy in 1552, made vicar general on the death of Ignatius in 1556, and was elected Ignatius' successor as general in 1558. He died in 1565.

[25] Alfonso Salmerón was born on September 6, 1515, in Toledo. He went to Alcalá to study, and there he met Diego Laínez. Together they went to Paris to find Ignatius. Salmerón was papal theologian at the Council of Trent (1546, 1551, and 1562) and was provincial of the Naples province (1558–1576). He died in Naples in 1585.

attend the entire course as long as he was able to find bread and water to keep himself alive. Once he had made this promise all those devout thoughts, which were coming to him at the wrong time, left him, and he quietly went on with his studies. During this period he was carrying on conversations with Master Pierre Favre and Master Francis Xavier, both of whom he later won to God's service through the Exercises.

At this juncture in his studies, no one was harassing him as previously. With reference to this, Doctor Frago once told him that he was surprised that he was quietly getting along without anyone causing him any trouble. He replied: "The

previously been students at the University of Alcalá, and because they had heard much about the Ignatius who once had been there, they decided to go to Paris and find this remarkable man. They arrived in Paris in early 1533. The last of Ignatius' first companions was Nicolás Bobadilla,[26] who came to the French capital in the fall of 1533 to continue his study of languages.

It was only in 1534, after he had six companions—all imbued with the same vision—that Ignatius took them through the Exercises. Favre spent January in retreat, then during the spring Laínez and Salmerón followed, then Rodrigues and Bobadilla. Xavier made the Exercises in September of that year. It may at first seem strange that of these companions Ignatius mentions only Favre and Xavier, but he recalls these not only because they were his roommates when he first went to Sainte-Barbe but also because both had already died—Favre in Rome (1546) and Xavier off the coast of China (1552).

---

[26] Nicolás Bobadilla's true name was Nicolás Alonso y Pérez, but he is known as Bobadilla because it was there that he was born about 1509. He studied at Valladolid, then went to Alcalá, where he earned his bachelor's degree in 1529. He returned to Valladolid to teach logic, while he studied theology for four years. He decided to go to Paris to study Latin, Greek, and Hebrew, and arrived there in the fall of 1533, when he met Ignatius. As a Jesuit he proved to be a tireless worker: in Germany (1542–1548), in Italy (1548–1558), in Valtellina (1558–1559), in Dalmatia (1559–1561), in Italy (1561–1590). He died in Loreto in 1590, the last of the first Jesuits.

reason is because I do not speak to anyone of the things of God, but when the course is over, I will return to it as usual."

83. While both of them were talking together, a friar came to ask Doctor Frago if he would find him a house, because in the house where he had a room many had died, from the plague he thought, for the plague was then beginning to spread in Paris. Doctor Frago and the pilgrim wanted to go and see the house, and they took a woman with them who understood these matters. After she went in, she confirmed that it was the plague. The pilgrim also wanted to enter, and finding the sick person, he comforted him and touched his

Ignatius' years in Paris, after the tumult caused by the change in Castro and Peralta, were calm and serene. Doctor Jerónimo Frago,[27] a professor of Scripture at the Sorbonne and a friend of Ignatius, had remarked about this in talking to him. Ignatius still intended to search out more disciples, but not during the school year.

83. The plague to which Ignatius refers is the one that began in Paris in 1531 but which did not become critical until August 1533, when institutions closed and people fled the city.[28] Since he says his visit to the house was at the time when the plague was beginning to spread, this may have been in 1531 or early 1532. After Ignatius had visited and touched the stricken individual, his imagination began to play tricks on him, and he felt certain that he had contracted the plague. On this occasion Ignatius followed his principle of *vince teipsum*, that is, by embracing something that is naturally repugnant we overcome the repugnance. Indeed, by touching the afflicted man and putting his hand into his mouth, Ignatius may have manifested heroism of spirit, but was his action in accord with

---

[27] Jerónimo Frago y Gárces was born in Uncastillo in the diocese of Pamplona. He received his master's degree in Paris in 1521, taught philosophy 1521–1525, and in 1529 began teaching Scripture at the Sorbonne. He received his doctor's degree in 1533 and died while a canon in Pamplona in 1537.

[28] So widespread was the plague during the summer of 1533 that Parlement issued ordinances on September 13, dealing with the problem. See *FX* 191.

sore with his hand. After he had consoled and encouraged the man a bit, he departed alone. He began to feel pain in his hand, and it seemed to him that he had the plague. This fantasy was so strong that he could not banish it until he thrust his hand into his mouth, turning it around this way and that, and said: "If you have the plague in your hand, you will also have it in your mouth." And as soon as he had done this the fantasy vanished as did the pain in his hand.

84. But when he returned to the Collège de Sainte-Barbe, where he was then living and following courses, those in the college, who knew that he had been in a house infected with the plague, ran from him and would not permit him to enter, and, thus, he was forced to remain outside for a few days.

There is a custom in Paris that the students in their third year of liberal arts, in order to receive the baccalaureate degree, must "take the stone", as they say, and since this costs an *escudo*, some of the very poor students are unable to do this. The pilgrim doubted whether it would be good for

the virtue of prudence? Ignatius was still in the process of learning, and later in life he would not have acted as he had done that day in Paris.[29]

84. At the university the philosophy course lasted three and a half years, but at the completion of the first two years the student was eligible for the bachelor's degree; after the full three and a half years, he was eligible for the licentiate degree. In January 1532, having completed his two years, Ignatius stood as a candidate for his first degree. The students referred to this as "taking the stone". The precise meaning of this Parisian phrase has never been preserved, but it has been suggested that that expression may also describe the custom in use at the University of Coimbra when a student presented himself for a degree. The candidate went before several examiners, and while the latter sat in their professorial chairs, the candidate sat on a stone in front of each examiner and answered the questions

---

[29] See *PY* 251–52 n. 31.

him to take it. Finding himself in a state of uncertainty and with no solution, he determined to place the matter in the hands of his teacher, who advised him to take it, and so he took it. Nonetheless, there were those who criticized him, and at least one Spaniard passed remarks about it.

About this time during his stay in Paris, his stomach began to act up, so that every two weeks he had stomach pain that lasted a good hour and brought on a fever. On one occasion the pain lasted for sixteen or seventeen hours. By this

---

put to him.[30] When the candidate finished with one examiner, he then passed on to another, sitting on another stone, and so on. To sit on the stone in the professor's presence was meant to signify the student's inferiority in the presence of his master. That such an examination should carry the heavy fee of an *escudo* is somewhat understandable when we realize that the fee not only covered the necessary testimonial letters, but most of it was used to defray the banquet that the graduates, by custom in medieval universities, had to provide for their professors.

What led Ignatius to hesitate about taking the degree? He does not give any hint as to the nature of his doubt, but some have proposed that since Ignatius had determined to live poorly, he considered the payment of the fee as being contrary to his resolve.[31] Others say that his doubt arose because to him taking a degree was tantamount to seeking honors[32] and, thus, contrary to humility. In any case, the professor whom he approached, probably Master Peña, for some reason or other encouraged him to take the degree.

At the time when Ignatius received his bachelor's degree, he was working toward his licentiate and successfully passed these examinations on March 13, 1533.[33] Ignatius was now ready to begin his program in theology, and in October he started his theological course with the Dominicans at Saint-Jacques.

---

[30] See *OC* 144 n. 24; *PY* 252 n. 32. *GV* 327 states that the university statutes directed that the students undergoing examination be given a hard seat.

[31] See *IL* 142.

[32] See *OC* 144 n. 24.

[33] See *FD*, doc. 84.

time he had already completed his liberal arts course and had studied theology for a couple of years and had gathered companions. His affliction was growing worse, and he was unable to find any remedy, though he had tried many.

85. The physicians kept saying that there was nothing that could benefit him more than the air of his homeland. Furthermore, his companions gave him the same advice, and they did it with some urgency. By this time they had all

During these final months of study the pain in his stomach returned; it was never accurately diagnosed, and it remained with him until his death.[34]

85–86. As a consequence of praying the Exercises, each of Ignatius' companions was more committed to God than before. Each now desired to be a priest and to spend his life in bringing spiritual benefit to other souls. To strengthen their companionship and to make visible their unity of heart and mind, the seven companions decided to take private vows of chastity, of poverty—to be practiced when they had completed their studies—and to go to Jerusalem to work for the conversion of the Turks. If unable to remain in the Holy Land, or if after a year's wait in Venice they were unable to go to the Holy Land, they would then go to Rome and place themselves at the disposal of the Holy Father. The date chosen for these vows was Saturday, August 15, 1534, the feast of the Assumption of our Lady.

Early that morning, shortly after sunrise and unnoticed by the Parisians, the seven companions made their way up to the Montmartre section of the city. They met at a prearranged spot and together they advanced to the chapel of Saint-Denis. The chapel was under the care of the Benedictine nuns and was believed to mark the spot where Saint Denis, the first Bishop of Paris, and his companions, Saints Rusticus and

---

[34] PY 253 identifies Ignatius' trouble as "biliary calculus, or chronic cholecystitis associated with gall stones". There Brodrick gives a quotation from Realdo Colombo, the surgeon who embalmed Ignatius shortly after his death, in which the surgeon states that he had taken from Ignatius' body numerous stones of various colors found in the kidneys, lungs, liver, and portal vein. See also Hugo Rahner, *Ignatius, the Man and the Priest* (Rome: Centrum Ignatianum Spiritualitatis, 1977), 99–105, where he treats Ignatius' physical ailments.

decided on what they would do, that is, go to Venice and Jerusalem and spend their lives there helping souls; and if permission be not granted them to remain in Jerusalem, they would return to Rome and offer themselves to the Vicar of Christ so that he could use them wherever he judged it would be for the greater glory of God and the good of souls. They had likewise made plans to wait an entire year in Venice before sailing. If there were no sailings to the East that year they would be free of their vow of going to Jerusalem and would go and see the pope.

Eleutherius, were martyred in the third century.[35] In the chapel's dimly lit crypt Favre, the only priest in the group—he had been ordained the previous May—celebrated the Mass. Before receiving Holy Communion, each, in turn, pronounced his vows as the group had planned. Ignatius was the eldest of the seven, being forty-three years old; the youngest was Salmerón, a mere nineteen. This event bound the seven together into a fellowship based on a common ideal and mutual love, but as yet they had no thought of forming a religious congregation. What took place in the crypt that morning was only the seed of what would eventually blossom into the Society of Jesus.

Ignatius and his companions continued in their study of theology with the Dominicans, and then on March 14, 1535, Ignatius was granted his master's diploma, entitling him to be known henceforth as Master Ignatius.[36] During these past few months of study Ignatius' health had been growing progressively worse, and the attacks he suffered were becoming more frequent. Though he did not want to interrupt his studies, nevertheless the physicians he consulted, as well as his companions, all agreed that since medical remedies proved ineffective, the only hope for him was to return to Azpeitia, where his native air might accomplish what medicine had failed to do. The visit to Spain would also give Ignatius the

---

[35] The crypt of Saint-Denis, 9 rue Antoinette, is now cared for by the Auxiliatrices.

[36] Text of this decree may be found in *FD*, doc. 86. For an English translation, see *PY* 254.

In the end, the pilgrim let his companions persuade him, and also because those who were Spaniards had some business that he could settle for them. They all agreed that after he got better he was to attend to their business and then leave for Venice and there wait for his companions.

86. That was in the year 1535, and according to their plan the companions were to set out in 1537, on the feast of the Conversion of Saint Paul. But because war had broken out, they set out in November 1536. Being about to depart, the pilgrim learned that an accusation had been brought before the inquisitor and that a process was being initiated against him. Knowing this fact, although they were not summoning

opportunity to visit the families of the Spaniards in his group and inform the families of the manner of life their sons had chosen to follow. He could assure them that all was well and that they ought not put any trust in rumors they might have heard coming from Paris. Ignatius also wanted to see his friends Arteaga, Calixto, Castro, and Peralta, for he still harbored the hope that they might now join his group.

Since Ignatius was soon to leave them, the companions decided that they would leave Paris on January 25, 1537, to meet Ignatius in Venice, and then the group could make its way to Jerusalem. Toward the end of March 1535 Ignatius was again denounced to the Inquisition because he continued to give the Exercises to those requesting them and because his group regularly attended services at the Carthusian monastery[37] and went to confession and received Communion every week. Though he had not been summoned, Ignatius, nevertheless, went to visit the inquisitor, talked to him, and asked that his case be adjudicated as soon as possible, since he was about to depart for Spain. The inquisitor, Valentín Liévin,[38] assured him that nothing serious had been brought against him, but having heard about his book, the Exercises, he very much wanted to see it. Ignatius supplied him with a copy, and when Liévin had read through it and found

---

[37] For Ignatius' relations with the Carthusians in Paris, see André Ravier, "Ignace de Loyola et la Chartreuse de Paris", *Christus* 42 (1995): 228–35.

[38] See *OC* 147 n. 30.

him, he himself went to the inquisitor and told him what he had heard, that he was about to depart for Spain, and that he had companions. So he asked him to pass sentence. The inquisitor said that with regard to an accusation being brought, that was true, but it did not appear to be anything important. He only wanted to see his writings, the Exercises. When he saw them he praised them highly and asked the pilgrim to leave a copy with him, and this he did. Nonetheless, he [the pilgrim] insisted that the process be carried out to the sentencing. Since the inquisitor offered excuses, he [the pilgrim] returned to his [the inquisitor's] residence with witnesses and a public notary, who took down everyone's testimony.

nothing in it that merited censure, he praised it, and as far as he was concerned the case was over. But Ignatius did not want to leave any suspicion hanging over his companions while he was away, and hence he asked that a favorable sentence be given. The inquisitor was reluctant to do so, thinking it not necessary, but Ignatius hired his own public notary, brought him and a few witnesses to the Dominican monastery where the inquisitor lived, and there the notary recorded the inquisitor's approval of Ignatius, of his group, and of the Exercises. Ignatius was now free to leave Paris and to return to Azpeitia; he had not seen his home for thirteen years.

Chapter 9

Spain: A Return Visit Home

(April–December 1535)

87. After he had completed this, he mounted the small horse his companions had purchased for him and set out alone for his homeland. On the way he found that he was feeling better. When he arrived in his province, he left the main road and took the mountain road because it was less traveled. After traversing a short distance he noticed two armed men coming toward him (that road is well known for its assassins), and after they had passed him by, they turned around and came rushing after him so that he was

87. In early April 1535, shortly after Easter (March 28), Ignatius left Paris to return to Spain; his constant companion on the trip was the small horse that his friends insisted he take because of his poor health. Since Ignatius followed the route that passed through Bayonne, which was one of the major stops on the way to Santiago de Compostela, it is probable that he had followed the pilgrim route ever since leaving Paris.[1] He crossed into Spain at Irún, and being within the borders of his home province of Guipúzcoa, he left the highway for the side roads that would take him

[1] PY 278 suggests that after leaving Paris, Ignatius passed through Chartres, Tours, Poitiers, Angoulême, and Bordeaux before reaching Bayonne. The distance from Paris to Azpeitia would be about five hundred miles, and it would have taken him about a month to traverse.

somewhat afraid. Nevertheless, he spoke to them and learned that they were his brother's servants and that his brother had despatched them to find him, since his brother had received news of his coming, it seems, from Bayonne in France, where someone had recognized the pilgrim. As they went on ahead, he followed along the same road. He met the aforementioned men traveling toward him a little before arriving in his home territory. The men stubbornly insisted that they take him to his brother's house, but they were unable to convince him to go. He thus went to the hospital, and when it was convenient for him, he went out to seek alms in the region.

through the mountains. This way he would not only enjoy the undulating landscapes of his beloved homeland, but he would be less likely to meet anyone who might recognize him. When he encountered the two armed servants, he was indeed glad to learn that they were not cutthroats but was surprised that the news of his coming had already reached his brother, Martín García, at Loyola Castle. Unknown to Ignatius, he had been recognized in Bayonne,[2] and the news was speedily sent back to his family. Since Ignatius was returning to Azpeitia as a pilgrim and not as the courtier he once had been, he declined to live in the ancestral castle and chose to stay in the humble Hospital de la Magdalena, a hospice for the poor on the outskirts of Azpeitia.[3] In exchange for lodging he gave them his horse.[4]

---

[2] Neither *OC* nor *FN* identifies the individual who recognized Ignatius in Bayonne; however, *IL* 158 and *GV* 372 identify him as Joán de Eguibar, a supplier of meat to the markets in Azpeitia.

[3] The tradition in Azpeitia, based on testimony given prior to Ignatius' beatification, is that he arrived on Friday, April 23. See *GV* 372–73 and Ignacio M. Zavala, "¿Convivió Ignacio de Loyola con leprosos durante su estancia en el hospital de la Magdalena de Azpeitia?" *Manresa* 67 (1995): 71–78.

[4] Sixteen years later, when Francis Borgia came to Azpeitia in January 1552, he stopped at this same hospice and found that the horse was still there. The horse is described as a nag (*cuartago*), "very fat and in good condition" (*OC* 148 n. 3; *FN* 1:482 n. 3).

88. At this hospital he began to speak about the things of God to the many individuals who came to visit him, and through God's grace much fruit resulted. No sooner had he arrived than he decided to teach Christian doctrine to the children daily, but his brother especially opposed this idea, saying no one would come. He replied that one would be enough. But after he had begun teaching, many continually came to hear him, as did his brother.

Besides teaching Christian doctrine, he used to preach on Sundays and feast days with benefit and profit to the souls

88–89. In Azpeitia Ignatius returned to his earlier practice of daily catechism for the children, and since adults were also coming, he arranged to speak to them three times a week. Because his explanation of the faith proved to be popular, they soon became daily instructions; and since the number of people attending was ever growing, he moved his talks from the hospital into the open air. On Sundays and feast days he preached in the church.[5] There are two reasons for Ignatius' popularity. First, the faithful in Azpeitia were starving for the food of the soul; sermons were rarely heard in the parish church, though there were some dozen priests associated with it.[6] Second, when Ignatius spoke about God and the things of God, he not only did so with sincerity and conviction, but it was evident to the people that he himself had experienced God, and the flames that had engulfed his heart also ignited theirs.

Though Ignatius spent only three months in Azpeitia, he accomplished much, not only in feeding the people with spiritual food, but also in seeing that certain pious customs were initiated and certain abuses eliminated. To assist the poor who were ashamed to beg, Ignatius persuaded the city magistrate and town council to draw up ordinances providing for the regular distribution of food for the poor.[7] An ordinance was also passed that church bells be rung at the time of the *Angelus* to remind the towns-

---

[5] See *GV* 373.

[6] See *IL* 167.

[7] These ordinances, dated May 23, 1535, may be found in *FD*, doc. 88. They state "that the poor would be regularly provided for out of public funds". See also *GV* 384–87.

who came many miles to hear him. He also tried to elimi-
nate some abuses, and with God's help he corrected some of
them. For example, he persuaded the magistrate of justice to
ban gambling and to see that the law was observed. There
was still another abuse, and it was this: the young girls of that
region always go about with heads uncovered and only cover
their heads when they marry. But there are many women
who have become mistresses to priests and to other men and
are faithful to them as if they were their wives. This practice
is so common that these mistresses have not the least shame
in saying that they have covered their heads for so and so and
are accepted as so and so's wife.

people to pray for those in mortal sin.[8] As for the abuses he helped elim-
inate, the first was gambling,[9] to which the people of Azpeitia were especially addicted and which was the cause of some of the poverty in that
area. He also helped terminate a custom that made shameful concubinage
socially acceptable.[10]

Sometime during his stay Ignatius' chronic stomach pain returned with
its usual fever. Once it had passed, he thought it time to move on and
fulfill the requests that his companions had made of him to visit their

---

[8] See GV 378. Ignatius' brother Martín García left a legacy in his will for
the bell ringers, so that the bells might continue to be rung daily for this
intention (FN 1:486 n. 8). Also on May 18, through Ignatius' mediation, the
controversy between the parish clergy of Azpeitia and the nuns of the Convent of the Immaculate Conception was brought to a peaceful end (FD, doc.
87).

[9] In his letter (August-September 1540) to the citizens of Azpeitia, Ignatius
reminds them to do without card playing and that there should be a prohibition on the sale of playing cards. See LIL 44.

[10] In the same letter Ignatius asks the citizenry of Azpeitia to put an end to
the practice of women who were not actually married wearing the headdress
of the married (LIL 44). In his letter (September 1539) to his nephew Beltrán,
who succeeded Martín García as master of Loyola, Ignatius asks him to continue to see to the reform of the clergy especially in Azpeitia, since that parish
church was under the patronage of the Loyola family (LIL 39). See GV 378–80.

89. Such a custom breeds many evils. The pilgrim persuaded the governor to pass a law that all who had covered their heads for someone and were not their wives should be punished according to the demands of justice. In this way the abuse began to be eliminated. He saw that an ordinance was passed so that the poor would be regularly provided for out of public funds and that the bells be rung three times a day at the *Ave Maria*, that is, in the morning, at noon, and in the evening, so that the people can pray as they do in Rome.

Although he at first had been in good health, he later on became critically ill. Once his health returned, he decided to set out to fulfill the tasks that his companions had entrusted to him and to go without any *quattrini*. His brother was greatly disturbed at this decision and was embarrassed that he wanted to go on foot. By the time evening came, the pilgrim had agreed to this: to travel to the provincial border on horseback and together with his brother and relatives.

90. But when he passed the province boundary he dismounted and, taking nothing with him, headed for Pamplona; and from there to Almazán, the hometown of Father

---

families and then to make his way to Italy, where he hoped to continue his study of theology while waiting for his companions to arrive. When Martín García learned that Ignatius was about to leave and intended to travel on foot and without money, he was embarrassed. To him it was unthinkable that a Loyola should thus publicly shame the family name. A Loyola had to travel on horse and with a retinue. Rather than cause his brother undue distress and in order to preserve peace, Ignatius finally yielded— but only to this degree: that as long as he was traveling within the confines of Guipúzcoa, he would do so on horse and with an entourage.

90. In late July Ignatius said good-by to his brother, whom he was never to see again, and continued his journey penniless and on foot. He was on his way to Obanos to deliver a letter to Juan de Azpilcueta,

Laínez; then to Sigüenza and Toledo; and from Toledo to Valencia. In all these hometowns of his companions he would not take anything, though a great deal was offered to him and with great insistence.

Xavier's brother,[11] but before reaching Obanos he had to pass through Pamplona. Gazing at the city ramparts, he remembered what had happened there fourteen years before and thanked God, who always works in mysterious ways, for calling him unto Himself. After delivering Xavier's letter, he walked southward to Almazán to Laínez' family, who rejoiced when they heard that their son was to become a priest. In their joy they offered Ignatius money and a horse for his travels, but these he politely refused.[12] He then went farther south to Sigüenza to meet some unknown acquaintance, then toward Madrid. Since the royal family was in residence, Ignatius paid a visit to Doña Leonor Mascarenhas, still acting as governess to the youthful Prince Philip, who, fifty years later as Philip II, remembered that he had once met the pilgrim.[13] In Madrid he surely visited Arteaga, who was tutor to the son of Don Juan de Zúñiga, Commander of Castile.[14] Ignatius still hoped to add his earlier companions to his group, but in this he had no success.

Ignatius then visited Toledo to see Salmerón's family[15] as well as Master Peralta (see no. 78), now associated with the church in that city. He continued his journey in a southeasterly direction until he came to Valencia and learned that Master Castro (see no. 78) had recently entered the

---

[11] See GV 393–94.

[12] See GV 395.

[13] See OC 150 n. 7; GV 395-96. In 1586, thirty years after Ignatius' death, as the artist Alonso Sánchez Coello was showing some of his more recent works to Philip II, the king recognized one of the portraits and remarked: "That one is very good; it looks just like him. I knew Fr. Ignatius and this is his face; but, when I knew him he had more of a beard."

[14] See OC 150 n. 7.

[15] See GV 396. Of the four Spaniards in his group, Ignatius visited the relatives of three of them (Xavier, Salmerón, and Laínez), but it seems that he did not visit those of Bobadilla. Bobadilla's father had died in 1517, and IL 178 suggests that perhaps his mother was also dead by this time.

In Valencia he spoke with Castro, who was a Carthusian monk. He wanted to board ship for Genoa, but his devoted friends in Valencia begged him not to, because they said that Barbarossa was at sea with his many galleys, and so on. Though they had told him enough things to frighten him, still, nothing could make him change his mind.

91. He boarded a large vessel and lived through the storm previously mentioned, when he said that he had been three times at the point of death.

When he arrived in Genoa, he took the road to Bologna, and on his way he suffered a great deal, especially on one occasion when he lost his way and began to walk alongside a river; the river was far below while the path was high above it. The farther he walked along the path, the narrower it became. It became so narrow that he could neither go ahead

Carthusian Order. Ignatius visited him at the Charterhouse of Val de Cristo and was a guest of the monastery for eight days and then went to live with Martín Pérez de Almazán, Castro's friend.[16] It was now November and time for Ignatius to look to Italy. When his Valencian friends heard that he was planning on taking ship to Genoa, they tried their utmost to dissuade him, telling him that the waters off Spain were infested with the ships of that red-bearded pirate Khair ed-Din,[17] more popularly known in and around the Mediterranean as Barbarossa. But no matter what they told him or how urgently they insisted, Ignatius would not change his plans because of fear.

91. Ignatius boarded the ship for Genoa, but while at sea the ship met a storm of such severity that its rudder was broken (see no. 33), and all aboard felt certain that they were to die at sea. Through God's providence the damaged vessel landed in Genoa in mid-November, and Ignatius immediately started on his 180-mile journey to Bologna. Since that city boasted

---

[16] See *FN* 1:186 n 12; *GV* 397 n. 43.

[17] Khird was a Barbary pirate and had adopted the name "Khair ed-Din" as an honorific title. He became admiral of the sultan's fleet in 1533 and died in 1546.

nor turn around to go back. He began to crawl on all fours, and in this fashion he covered a good distance, but with much fear, because every time he moved he thought he was going to fall into the river. This was the greatest physical strain and exertion he had ever experienced, but in the end he made it. As he was about to enter Bologna and was crossing over a small wooden bridge, he fell off of it. Thus, as he arose covered with mud and water he made the bystanders break out in laughter.

He entered Bologna and began to beg alms but received not even a single *quattrino*, though he had tried everywhere. He stayed in Bologna for some time because he was ill, then he went to Venice, always traveling in the same manner.

of a famous university, and the school year had just begun, Ignatius thought of spending the coming year there continuing his study of theology. On his way to Bologna he somehow lost his way, and on one occasion, as he was crossing the Apennines, he found himself traveling an extremely narrow path that hugged the edge of a cliff. Successfully extricating himself from that predicament, he continued until he was on the city's outskirts. As he was crossing a footbridge he slipped and fell into the cold muddy water below. In mud-covered clothes, Ignatius made his entrance into that famous city, but his every attempt at begging proved unsuccessful. He did learn where the Spanish College was located—it was named San Clemente[18]—and there his countrymen gave him food and lodging. In mid-December he again suffered from acute pain in the stomach, so much so that he remained bedridden for a week. When he finally recovered he realized that it was the Bolognese climate that was causing him distress, so he relinquished the idea of studying at the university and judged it better to go on to Venice. Thus, he set out after Christmas[19] and arrived in Venice at the end of 1535.

---

[18] See *FN* 1:188 n. 10; *GV* 399–400. The Spanish College was founded in 1364 by Cardinal Gil Carillo de Albornoz.

[19] See *FN* 1:188 n. 13; *GV* 400.

Chapter 10

Venice and Vicenza: Awaiting Passage to the Holy Land

(January 1536–November 1537)

92. During his time in Venice he occupied himself giving the Exercises and in other spiritual conferences. The more illustrious persons to whom he gave them were Master Pietro Contarini and Master Gasparo de Dotti, and a Spaniard

92. In Venice Ignatius stayed with Andrea Lippomani,[1] prior of La Santissima Trinità, a poor but holy and learned man. Since Venice had no university of its own—Venetian students attended that of Padua, some twenty-three miles away—Ignatius continued his study of theology privately, and in addition to the books that he had bought for himself, he enjoyed the use of Lippomani's excellent library. Besides studying, he was also engaged in carrying on spiritual conversations with clergy and lay persons and in giving the Exercises to those whom he judged ready. Among the several whom Ignatius had led through the Exercises, he mentions

---

[1] On February 12, 1536, Ignatius wrote to Jaime Cassador, archdeacon of the cathedral of Barcelona, to inform him that he had been in Venice for a month and a half and that he was enjoying the hospitality and friendship of a very good and learned man (*LIL* 15). Ignatius does not identify his host, but *PY* 293, *FX* 300, and *GV* 401 think it was Andrea Lippomani. See also Angelo Martini, "Di chi fu ospite S. Ignacio a Venezia nel 1536?" *Archivum Historicum Societatis Iesu* 18 (1949): 253–60. On the other hand, *IL* 183 thinks Ignatius' host may have been Martín de Zornoza, the Spanish consul in Venice.

whose name was Rozas. There was also another Spaniard named Bachelor Hoces, who had many dealings with the pilgrim and also with the Bishop of Chieti. And though he had some inclination to make the Exercises, still, he did not

four. Master Pietro Contarini[2] was a noble Venetian cleric whose family had given several doges to the Venetian Republic, and Master Gasparo de Dotti[3] was vicar general to Girolamo Verallo, papal legate in Venice. The Spaniard Rozas[4] remains unidentified, and Bachelor Hoces,[5] another Spaniard, was friendly with Ignatius and with Gian Pietro Carafa, co-founder of the Theatines and Bishop of Chieti.[6] That Hoces was at first reluctant to make the Exercises is perhaps attributable to Carafa, who heart-ily disliked Spaniards because, as a Neapolitan, he did not appreciate their

---

[2] Pietro Contarini was procurator at the hospital for the incurably ill in Ven-ice. In 1557 he was appointed Bishop of Paphos in Cyprus and resigned that see in 1562. Together with Cardinal Gasparo Contarini, a relative of his, he was of great assistance to the young Society. He died in Padua in 1563. See *OC* 152 n. 1.

[3] Gasparo de Dotti's name appears in the original text as de Doctis, that is, in its Latin form. When he became acquainted with Ignatius, he was con-nected with the papal legate in Venice. In 1551 he was made governor of Loreto, and in 1556 was permitted to take simple vows in the Society while remaining, at Ignatius' recommendation, in charge of the sanctuary. He died in Loreto in 1563. See *OC* 152 n. 2; *FX* 304 n. 79.

[4] *OC* 153 n. 3 indicates that it is not certain who this individual was, but following *FN* 1:490 n. 3 it suggests that it might have been a certain Rodrigo Rozas. See *GV* 409–10.

[5] Diego de Hoces was born in Málaga and was in Venice because he had only recently returned from the Holy Land. His death in March 1538 may have been the result of his caring for the plague-stricken. See *OC* 153 n. 4; *PY* 295 n. 8.

[6] The text refers to a Bishop of Cette, but since there is no diocese by that name, some have suggested that it should be Ceuta in Mauritania. This is un-likely, however (see *OC* 154 n. 5). More probably the name should be Chieti, for its bishop, Gian Pietro Carafa, was then residing in Venice. In 1524, together with Saint Cajetan of Theine, Carafa founded the Congregation of Clerks Reg-ular. Carafa was the congregation's first superior, and because he had been Bishop of Chieti (*Theate* in Latin), members of that congregation were known as The-atines. During the sack of Rome in 1527, the Theatines were banished and found refuge in Venice, where Carafa remained until September 1536, when he was called to Rome. On December 22 of that year Pope Paul III made him a cardinal.

do anything about it. He finally decided to begin making them, and three or four days into them, he opened his soul to the pilgrim, telling him that, because of the things someone had told him, he was afraid that some villainous doctrine would be taught him in the Exercises. This was why he had brought certain books with him so that he could refer to them if, by chance, anyone wanted to deceive him. He was singularly helped by the Exercises, and at the end he decided to follow the pilgrim's manner of life. He was also the first to die.

having control of his native land, and it seems that he likewise bore a special animosity toward Ignatius himself.[7] Hoces finally made the Exercises and realized that all that had been told him about Ignatius and the Exercises was untrue, and, thus, he joined Ignatius' enterprise. He died in early 1538 while preaching in Padua, and Ignatius, involved in giving the Exercises at Monte Cassino (see no. 98), saw his soul enter heaven.

---

[7] The reason for Carafa's supposed animosity toward Ignatius has never been uncovered. Sometime in 1536, Ignatius composed a letter, presumably addressed to Carafa, in which he politely offered suggestions on how Carafa's con gregation could better itself. Ignatius finds fault with the members not begging, preaching, or practicing the corporal works of mercy. Was the letter actually sent to Carafa? There are some who think not, e.g., *GV* 410–14 and Georges Bottereau, "La 'lettre' d'Ignace de Loyola à Gian Pietro Carafa", *Archivum Historicum Societatis Iesu* 44 (1975): 139–51. If sent, then Ignatius' observations would not have been well received. Carafa might have viewed the letter as coming from someone who was his junior, attempting to instruct him on how the Theatine congregation should be managed. Furthermore, Ignatius was not yet ordained, nor was he a member of any religious congregation. (For the text of Ignatius' letter, see *LIL* 28–31). On the death of Pope Marcellus II in 1555, Carafa, then in his seventy-ninth year, was elected to the papacy on May 23 and took the name Paul IV. When Ignatius heard this news, it is said that his jaw fell and that he immediately went to the chapel to pray. When he returned he appeared as happy as if his closest friend had been elected pope (*FN* 1:581–82). For a discussion of the difference in thinking between Ignatius and the cardinal, see Victor Codina, "San Ignacio y Paulo IV: Notas para un teología del carisma", *Manresa* 40 (1968): 337–62, especially 340–45. Also his "Espérant contre toute espérance: Ignace et Paul IV", *Christus* 17 (1970): 99–107.

93. The pilgrim suffered another persecution while in Venice, with many saying that his effigy had been burned in Spain and in Paris. This affair reached such a point that he was brought to trial, and a sentence, favorable to the pilgrim, was given.

93. It appears that Ignatius was reluctant to reveal the name of the individual responsible for this persecution. Jerónimo Nadal, however, indicates in a letter that "opposition [against Ignatius], spurred on by Pietro Carafa, arose in Venice."[8] Whether Carafa was the cause of this persecution remains doubtful, but when Ignatius gave his reasons for not going to Rome with his companions in the spring of 1537, the new Theatine cardinal—Carafa was named cardinal in December 1536—was one of them. The Venetian campaign against Ignatius ended with his being brought to trial, but the final sentence was in Ignatius' favor.[9]

While Ignatius was in Spain and Venice, his six companions in Paris had increased their number to nine. In 1535 Claude Jay,[10] a Savoyard,

---

[8] "Venetiis excitata est contradictio a Petro Caraffa." See *Epistolae Hieronymi Nadal* 4 (*MHSI*) (Madrid: Lopez del Horno, 1905), 706.

[9] Ignatius' detractors, whoever they were, had spread the rumor that he and his companions were fugitives from Spain and Paris, that they had been prosecuted in both cities, and that they had been burned in effigy. In view of these accusations, the papal legate, Girolamo Verallo, asked his vicar, Gasparo de Dotti, to initiate an investigation. After receiving the testimony of witnesses, the vicar issued his verdict on October 13, 1537, stating that Ignatius was to be declared innocent and that all that had been said against him was "frivolous, vain and false", and that Ignatius was a priest of sound doctrine, that he enjoyed a good reputation and that ever since his coming to Venice he had taught true doctrine and had given good example. See *FD*, doc. 105.

[10] Claude Jay was born between 1500–1504. As a youth he attended school with Pierre Favre at Collège de la Roche, Savoy. He was ordained a priest on March 28, 1528, and was conducting a small school when Favre visited him in 1533 and encouraged him to go to Paris to continue his studies. He arrived in Paris in October 1534, made the Exercises under Favre's direction, and pronounced his vows at Montmartre on August 15, 1535. As a Jesuit he labored in Italy (1537–1541) and in Germany (1542–1549). He attended the Council of Trent (1545–1547) and the diet of Augsburg (1550). He died in Vienna in 1551 as rector of the university in that city. See *FX* 260.

The nine companions arrived in Venice at the beginning of 1537. They split up so as to help in different hospitals. After two or three months they all went to Rome to obtain the blessing for their journey to Jerusalem. The pilgrim did

made the Exercises under Favre and joined the group, and in 1536 Paschase Broët[11] and Jean Codure[12] did the same. The original plan was that the group was to depart Paris for Venice on January 25, 1537, but since hostilities between France and Spain were renewed in 1536, and since Charles V had attacked Marseilles and had his forces in the Low Countries invade the north of France, the Parisians were filled with anti-Spanish sentiments. Since half of the companions were Spaniards, they decided to anticipate the date of their departure. The route to Italy through southern France was out of the question, and so they chose to go through the neutral Duchy of Lorraine and Germany. A circuitous route, to be sure, but a safer one. Half of them left on November 11, 1536, and went as far as Meaux to await the others. The remaining companions left the City of Light on November 15, met their friends at Meaux, and started their two-month journey. They entered Germany at Zabern, then took the road to Basel, Constance, Trent, and finally the nine arrived in Venice on January 8, 1537, two months ahead of schedule.[13]

Just as Favre had three new recruits (Jay, Broët, and Codure), to introduce to Ignatius, the latter also had three recruits to present to his newly

---

[11] Paschase Broët was born in Picardy, France, in 1500. He studied at Amiens and was ordained there in 1524. He spent the next ten years in a parish but then went to Paris in 1534. There he met Favre and made the Exercises and later pronounced his vows at Montmartre on August 15, 1536. As a Jesuit he labored in Siena (1537–1540), went with Salmerón as papal legate to Ireland (1541), and then labored in Italy (1542–1551). He was provincial in France (1552–1562) and died in Paris in 1562, while serving the plague-stricken. See FX 261–62.

[12] Jean Codure came from southern France and was born in 1508. He came to Paris and began his studies at the university in 1534. He placed himself under Favre's spiritual direction, made the Exercises, and took vows with Broët at Montmartre on August 15, 1536. Codure was the first of the companions to die in Rome; he died on August 29, 1541. See FX 263.

[13] For Rodrigues' account of the Paris to Venice trip, see GV 418–23.

not go because of Doctor Ortiz and also because of the new Theatine cardinal. The companions returned from Rome with drafts of two hundred or three hundred *escudos*, which had been given them as alms for their passage to Jerusalem. They

arrived friends. These new recruits of Ignatius were Diego de Hoces, and the Eguía brothers, Diego and Esteban. The latter two had recently returned from the Holy Land and unexpectedly found Ignatius, whom they had previously known in Alcalá (see no. 57). They made the Exercises under his supervision and then expressed their desire to join him after they had settled their affairs in Spain.[14] Since the group would have to wait for the pilgrim ship to take them to the Holy Land—and that was not due to come until sometime in June or July—the ten companions in Venice broke up into two groups and went to help in two of Venice's hospitals, that of Santi Giovanni e Paolo and that for the incurables.[15] Ignatius, however, remained tied to his books, since he was eager to finish his studies in time to be ordained before leaving for the Holy Land. The priests among them heard the confessions of the sick and prepared them for death, while the nonpriests busied themselves in sweeping floors, making beds, washing patients and bedpans, digging graves, and burying the dead. For two months they worked in the hospitals, and when March came it was time to seek papal approval for their pilgrimage to Jerusalem and to request ordination for the nonpriests among them.

The companions left Venice about March 10, desirous of being in the Eternal City for Holy Week and Easter.[16] Ignatius remained behind, thinking that his presence would only excite the ire of Cardinal Carafa, who

---

[14] Of the two brothers, Esteban was the elder and a widower, while Diego was already ordained. Both brothers set out for Spain before the companions began their work in Venice's hospitals. See n. 15 under chapter 6 above.

[15] Hoces, Rodrigues, Salmerón and two others assisted at Santi Giovanni e Paolo, while Favre, Xavier, Laínez, and two others were at the other hospital. See *GV* 424.

[16] According to Rodrigues' account, the companions followed the Adriatic down to Ravenna, where they arrived on the eighteenth. They spent two days there, then on to Ancona and to Loreto, where they likewise spent two days visiting the sanctuary. They then took the road to Tolentino, through Foligno and Terni, and entered Rome by crossing the Milvian Bridge (*GV* 424).

were unwilling to take anything except drafts, and later, when they were not able to go to Jerusalem, they returned the drafts to those who had given them.

The companions returned to Venice in the same way that they had gone, that is, on foot and begging their way, but they were divided in three groups, in such a way that each

was at the papal court, and Doctor Ortiz,[17] who was also in Rome. The companions arrived in Rome on Palm Sunday, March 25. They secured lodging at the Spanish hospice and met Doctor Ortiz, who, when he had been informed of the purpose of their visit, not only showed interest in their cause but also manifested great benevolence toward them, for it was he who informed the pope that several masters from the University of Paris were in the city seeking audience. In response to Doctor Ortiz' request, the pope immediately set April 3, Easter Tuesday, as the date for their meeting. The encounter in Castel Sant'Angelo was most pleasant, and the pope so genuinely enjoyed their conversation and discussion that when the audience was nearing its end he approved their pilgrimage, offered them sixty ducats to help pay their passage, and granted permission for the ordination of the nonpriests, but added that tension was growing in the Mediterranean so that they might never reach Jerusalem. Imitating the pope's generosity, the cardinals present likewise made offerings toward the pilgrimage, so that the net result of that meeting, together with gifts from others, was 210 ducats.[18] They left Rome at the beginning of May,[19] and when they arrived in Venice they returned to their volunteer work at

---

[17] Ortiz was the individual who, it is thought, had denounced Ignatius to the Inquisition in Paris over the Castro-Peralta affair (see no. 81). He had been in Rome since the end of 1530 as Charles V's agent assigned to defend the right of the emperor's aunt, Queen Catherine, against Henry VIII's attempt to divorce her. After the queen died on January 7, 1536, Pope Paul III asked him to remain in Rome as a special counselor.

[18] See *GV* 426.

[19] They carried two documents with them, both issued in Rome on April 27; one was the dimissorial letters for their ordination to the priesthood, except for Salmerón, who had not yet completed his twenty-second year (*FD*, doc. 101), and the other was papal permission for their pilgrimage to the Holy Land (*FD*, doc. 102).

group was made up of different nationalities. There in Venice, those who were not ordained were ordained for Mass, and the nuncio, who was then in Venice and who was later known as Cardinal Verallo, granted them faculties. They were ordained under the title of poverty, and everyone took vows of poverty and chastity.

94. Ships were not sailing to the East that year because the Venetians had broken off relations with the Turks. Seeing that the possibility of sailing was becoming more remote, they dispersed throughout the Veneto region to wait out the year as they had agreed, and if there were no sailing after the year had passed, they would go to Rome.

the hospitals. On June 24, Ignatius, with five others (Xavier, Laínez, Rodrigues, Bobadilla, and Codure), was ordained to the priesthood by Vincenzo Nigusanti, Bishop of Arbe in Dalmatia, but a resident of Venice.[20] Subsequently the nuncio, Girolamo Verallo,[21] granted the group extensive faculties permitting them to hear confessions, dispense sacraments, preach, and teach Scripture anywhere in the Venetian Republic.[22]

94. Since the Adriatic and Mediterranean were swarming with Turkish galleys, and since Venice was preparing for war with the sultan, it became increasingly unlikely that a pilgrim ship would be going to the Holy Land that summer. So the would-be pilgrims changed their plans and decided to wait until the following summer. In the meantime they prepared to celebrate their first Masses. The eleven of them broke up into groups of

---

[20] On June 10 they received the four minor orders, subdiaconate on the fifteenth, the diaconate on the seventeenth, with priesthood on the twenty-fourth. Salmerón received up to the diaconate, but he would have to wait a few more months for priesthood. All these orders were conferred in the bishop's private chapel in Venice. The titles under which they were ordained were "adequate knowledge" (*sufficientis scientiae*) and "voluntary poverty" (*voluntarie paupertatis*). See *FD*, doc. 103.

[21] Verallo was born about 1497 and had been nuncio in Venice from 1537 to February 1540. He became cardinal on April 8, 1549, and died on October 10, 1555.

[22] This document is dated July 5, 1537 (*FD*, doc. 104).

It fell to the pilgrim to go with Favre and Laínez to Vicenza. There they found a certain building outside the city that had neither doors nor windows. They stayed in it and slept on the bit of straw that they had brought. Twice a day two of them went out to seek alms in that locality, and they returned with so little that they could hardly sustain themselves. They usually ate some cooked bread—when they had bread—and the one who stayed at home took care of the cooking. In this way they spent forty days attending to nothing but their prayers.

95. After the forty days had passed, Master Jean Codure arrived, and the four of them decided to begin preaching. All four went to different squares in the city, and at the same

---

two and three and, choosing by lot, they went to several northern Italian cities to spend forty days in prayer prior to their Masses. But before leaving Venice, Ignatius returned to Doctor Ortiz the ducats collected in Rome and asked him to keep them until an opportunity for sailing would again present itself.[23] The companions left Venice on July 25, and Ignatius, Favre, and Laínez went to Vicenza, forty-three miles west of Venice. The others went to Monselice, Treviso, Bassano, and Verona.

About a mile beyond the Santa Croce gate of Vicenza, Ignatius and his little group came upon the abandoned monastery of San Pietro in Vivarolo,[24] and there they took up residence. That they had to go out and beg twice a day shows how little they collected on each attempt. Usually Ignatius remained at the monastery and prepared the meals of cooked bread;[25] he was again suffering from stomach pain, and his eyes had become weak because of the many tears he shed in prayer.[26]

95. The forty days in Vicenza were days of incessant prayer and of intimate union with God, and during that period Ignatius was the recipient

---

[23] See *OC* 155 n. 8; *FX* 347.

[24] See *OC* 156 n. 10.

[25] *PY* 316 n. 25 suggests that they were given only hard, moldy crusts that had to be boiled in order to become edible.

[26] See *FX* 360.

hour of the same day they began their sermons by shouting loudly to the people and waving their birettas to call them together. These sermons caused much talk in the city, and many persons were moved with devotion and abundantly supplied them with all that they materially needed.

During the period that he was in Vicenza, he received many spiritual visions and many rather ordinary consolations (it was just the opposite when he was in Paris), but especially when he began to prepare for his ordination in Venice and when he was getting ready to celebrate Mass.

of many extraordinary graces, similar to those he had received while in Manresa. Such graces had been granted him in Venice when he was preparing for his ordination and now in Vicenza as he was preparing to celebrate his first Mass. Toward the end of August, having received word from Bassano that Rodrigues was on his deathbed, Ignatius and Favre went to visit him.

The forty days were up on September 6, and shortly thereafter Codure joined them, coming from Treviso,[27] and all four went into the city to begin their apostolate of preaching. None of the four was fluent enough in Italian to be able to hold public discourse, but that did not deter them. Ignatius had been in Italy for eighteen months, and when he began his discourse it also included some French and Latin,[28] nevertheless, he and his companions made themselves understood so that the people not only became interested but returned to hear them and responded generously by giving them alms.

All ten companions eventually convened at the deserted monastery outside Vicenza to evaluate their present situation. Since there would be no pilgrim ship going to the Holy Land that year, they all determined to wait another year. What to do in the meantime? They were all university graduates, and so they decided to go to the various university centers in

---

[27] Codure had been in Treviso with Hoces. It seems that they had received word of Rodrigues' relapse (after Ignatius' visit), and feeling that Hoces could do more for Rodrigues than Jay, who knew no Portuguese, Hoces went to Bassano to be with them. Rather than remaining alone in Treviso, Codure went to Vicenza. See FX 360 n. 194.

[28] See FN 2:84.

Also during his journeys he enjoyed great supernatural visitations of the kind that he used to have when he was in Manresa. While he was in Vicenza he learned that one of the companions, who was in Bassano, was at the point of death. Though he himself was ill with fever at that time, nevertheless, he started on the trip and walked so energetically that Favre, his companion, could not keep up with him. During that trip God gave him the assurance, and this he told Favre, that the companion would not die from that illness. After he arrived at Bassano, the sick man was greatly consoled and quickly recovered.

Everyone then returned to Vicenza, and all ten were there for some time, and some went out begging alms in the towns around Vicenza.

96. They decided that after a year had passed, and if they still found no passage, they would go to Rome, and the pilgrim too, because the last time the companions had gone there the two men about whom he had had his doubts had shown themselves most benevolent.

Italy (Padua, Ferrara, Bologna, and Siena) and begin their apostolate of preaching and teaching, hearing confessions, and giving the Exercises, and so on. Perhaps they might win some new recruits from among the students. Ignatius, Favre, and Laínez were to go to Rome and do the same there.

Before dispersing, one final question had to be settled: If anyone should ask them to which congregation they belonged, or what they called themselves, what answer should they give? Ignatius suggested that they pray over it, and when the discussion was renewed, everyone acknowledged that since no one among them was their head, but only Jesus Christ, and since it was Jesus whom they desired to serve, they ought to carry His name. Thus they decided on calling themselves *Compañía de Jesús*, but when this was rendered into Latin it became *Societas Jesu*, and when this is translated into English it becomes the familiar *Society of Jesus*.

96–97. The others who were ordained with Ignatius in June had celebrated their first Masses in Vicenza sometime in September, but Ignatius

They went to Rome in three or four groups; the pilgrim was with Favre and Laínez, and on this journey God often visited him in a special way.

After he had been ordained a priest, he decided to wait another year before celebrating Mass, preparing himself and praying to our Lady to place him with her Son. One day, a

---

chose to postpone his for another year.[29] He still carried the hope that he might celebrate it in the Holy Land.

While waiting for the year to pass and hoping that the summer of 1538 would bring a pilgrim ship to Venice, the companions dispersed to the various cities while Ignatius went to Rome. He was no longer worried about Doctor Ortiz and Cardinal Carafa; the former had proven to be a friend when the companions visited Rome the previous year, and as for the latter, Ignatius had been vindicated in the trial that had been brought against him in Venice.

According to their revised plan, the companions were to spend the winter preaching in the cities assigned to them, and when spring came they were to go to Rome for further deliberation. Ignatius, Favre, and Laínez left Vicenza in October. This journey to Rome was Ignatius' final cross-country journey, and the three pilgrims, coming from Siena, approached Rome by the Via Cassia. About eight miles outside the city they came to the small village of La Storta. Since they were tired, but at the same time eager to get to Rome that evening, they chose to stop at the chapel, get some rest, do some praying, and then continue on their way. When Ignatius relates his mystical experience at La Storta, he merely gives the basic facts and omits all detail and embellishment.[30] But from those who were with him we learn that as soon as he entered the chapel he felt a sudden change come over him, and while he was praying he had a remarkable vision. He saw God the Father together with Jesus, who was carrying His cross. Both Father and Son were looking most kindly upon

---

[29] That is, Bobadilla, Codure, Laínez, and Xavier celebrated their first Masses. Rodrigues celebrated his in Ferrara, and Salmerón in Venice, where he was ordained at the end of October or the first days of November.

[30] See *FN* 2:133 n. 19; *GV* 438–41. Hugo Rahner, *The Vision of St. Ignatius in the Chapel of La Storta* (Rome: Centrum Ignatianum Spiritualitatis, 1975).

few miles before reaching Rome, while praying in a church, he felt a great change in his soul, and so clearly did he see God the Father place him with Christ, His Son, that he had no doubts that God the Father did place him with His Son.

97. Then on arriving in Rome he told the companions that he saw that the windows were closed, meaning by this that they would have to suffer many contradictions. He likewise said: "We must always be on our guard, and hold no conversations with women, unless they be ladies of prominence." Later in Rome, to continue on this same subject, Master Francis heard a woman's confession and once visited her to speak to her of spiritual matters. She was later found to be pregnant, but it pleased the Lord that the man who had done the wicked deed was discovered. The same happened to Jean Codure, whose spiritual daughter was caught with a man.

him, and he heard the Father say to the Son: "I wish you to take him as your servant." Jesus then directed His words to the kneeling pilgrim and said: "I wish you to be our servant." This was exactly what Ignatius had always wanted. Then he heard the Father add: "I will be favorable to you in Rome." This was God's answer to Ignatius' frequent prayer that he be placed next to Mary's Son. Leaving the chapel and continuing on his way to Rome, Ignatius did not know whether he would meet success or persecution, but he knew that God would be with him.

Upon entering Rome he noticed that the windows in the buildings were closed, and he interpreted this to mean that they would meet opposition and persecution, but having the assurance of divine protection, he knew those forces could not prevail over the Society of Jesus. Still, they were to be cautious, and Ignatius told them to be prudent when dealing with women. He then cited two examples of what had happened to Xavier and Codure shortly after their arrival in Rome. To avoid such embarrassment in the future, Ignatius decided that no one was to hear the confessions of women in their homes without a companion.[31]

---

[31] See *FX* 492.

Chapter 11

Rome: First Year in the Eternal City

(1538)

98. From Rome the pilgrim went to Monte Cassino to give the Exercises to Doctor Ortiz. He was there for forty days, and once during that period he saw Bachelor Hoces enter heaven, and as a result of this he shed many tears and

---

98. In Rome, Ignatius and his companions were offered the use of an empty house in the vineyard on the estate of Quirino Garzoni, and there they made their home.[1] The building was located on Monte Pincio, near the church Trinità dei Monti, where Favre and Laínez celebrated daily Mass. Pope Paul III, remembering that these were university-trained theologians, appointed Favre and Laínez to teach at Rome's Sapienza College, while he left Ignatius free to carry on his particular apostolate of preaching and giving the Exercises.[2] Among the first to make the Exercises was Doctor Ortiz, who was now one of Ignatius' most enthusiastic supporters.

---

[1] The house, though now remodeled and enlarged, still stands on Via San Sebastianello 11. See *FX* 408 n. 11.

[2] On December 19, 1538, Ignatius wrote to Isabel Roser: "It is more than a year since three of us . . . arrived here in Rome. . . . Two of us then began to teach without charging fees in the Sapienza College, the one positive theology [Favre], and the other scholastic theology [Laínez], and this by command of the Pope. I gave myself up entirely to giving and communicating the spiritual exercises to others, both in Rome and outside the city" (*LW* 270). The Sapienza had been founded in 1303 and had only recently reopened after the sack of Rome (1527).

had great spiritual consolation. He saw this so clearly that if he were to say the contrary he would feel as though he were lying. From Monte Cassino he brought back with him Francisco Estrada.

At the beginning of March 1538, Ignatius and Doctor Ortiz traveled the eighty-eight miles to Monte Cassino. In the nearby dependent priory of Santa Maria dell'Albaneta,[3] Ignatius and the Doctor prayed for forty days. On their return trip to Rome they met a young Spaniard whom Ignatius knew, Francisco Estrada,[4] who was on his way to Naples to join the military. Ignatius persuaded him to return to Rome, where he made the Exercises and eventually entered the Society. Among the others whom Ignatius led through the Exercises, the more prominent were Cardinal Gasparo Contarini,[5] who always remained a faithful friend of the Society, and the humanist ambassador from Siena, Lattanzio Tolomei.[6] There were others as well, scattered throughout Rome, and by mentioning that one retreatant lives near Santa Maria Maggiore and another by Ponte Sisto, Ignatius is telling us that each day he had to go from one end of the city to the other in order to lead his retreatants through their meditations.

Ignatius had asked all the companions to be in Rome for Easter, since it was almost certain that there would be war and that the chances of

---

[3] See FX 415 n. 55; GV 446–47.

[4] Francisco Estrada was a Spaniard, born about 1519 in Dueñas. He had studied in Alcalá and then had gone to Rome in 1526 to seek his fortune. Doctor Ortiz secured a position for him in the household of Cardinal Vincenzo Carafa. While Ignatius was at Monte Cassino, Cardinal Carafa dismissed the Spaniards in his household, and, thus, Estrada was on his way to Naples hoping to enlist in the Spanish forces. Having met Ignatius, he returned to Rome. As a Jesuit he was a renowned preacher in Italy, Belgium, Portugal, and Spain. He was rector at Burgos (1551–1554) and provincial (1554–1557). His health then began to fail, and he spent his final fifteen years living as a hermit in Toledo, where he died in 1584. See FX 417 n. 65; OC 160 n. 3; GV 447.

[5] Gasparo Contarini (1483-1542) was made cardinal in 1535 and had served as papal legate to Speyer (1540), Germany (1541), Bologna (1542), and to the emperor (1542). It was he who took the "Formula of the Institute" to Paul III. For a modern biography of the cardinal, see Elizabeth Gleason, Gasparo Contarini: Venice, Rome, and Reform (Berkeley: University of California, 1993).

[6] See GV 445.

When he returned to Rome he kept himself busy helping souls, and while still living at the vineyard he gave the Spiritual Exercises to several individuals at one and the same time. One of these lived near Santa Maria Maggiore and another near Ponte Sisto.

going to the Holy Land were becoming more and more remote. After they had arrived, the companions went to various churches in Rome and began their preaching. Ignatius went to that of Santa Maria di Monserrato, since this was the Spanish church and there he would be able to preach in Spanish.[7] The principal content of these sermons were the fundamentals of the Catholic faith, but with a view to correcting the Lutheran teaching that an Augustinian friar, Agostino Mainardi,[8] had expounded in his sermons during Lent. Since the companions were trying to undo the harm that Mainardi had done, some of the latter's followers—three Spaniards in the Roman Curia, Francisco de Mudarra, a certain Barreda, and Pedro de Castilla[9]—concocted vicious lies about Ignatius and his companions and planted them throughout the city. Thus began a persecution that Ignatius judged to be the most severe he had ever undergone.[10] The story was passed around that Ignatius and his companions were disguised Lutherans who, by the Exercises, intended to teach

---

[7] On May 3, 1538, Cardinal Vincenzo Carafa, papal legate for Rome, granted Ignatius and companions faculties to preach and exercise their ministry wherever they chose (*FD*, doc. 106). On May 5 they began their preaching: Favre at San Lorenzo in Damaso, Salmerón in Santa Lucia in Gonfalone, Rodrigues in Sant'Angelo in Pescheria, Bobadilla in San Celso e Giuliano, Laínez at San Salvatore in Lauro, and Jay at San Luigi dei Francesi. Xavier's broken health compelled him to remain at home (*GV* 448).

[8] For a thorough description of this persecution and the role that Mainardi's sermons played in it, see *FX* 419–42.

[9] See *FX* 421–22; *OC* 161 n. 7.

[10] In his letter of December 19, 1538, to Isabel Roser, Ignatius writes: "During eight months we have experienced the most severe persecution and hostility that we have ever undergone in this life. I do not mean that they have annoyed us in our persons, nor called us before the justices, nor ill-treated us in any other way; but by spreading rumours among the people and by unheard-of statements, they made us objects of suspicion and hatred to the people." For the complete letter with further details, see *LW* 269–74.

Then the persecutions began. Miguel started trouble by speaking ill of the pilgrim and had him summoned before the governor. The pilgrim first showed the governor one of Miguel's letters in which he enthusiastically praised him; the governor then interrogated Miguel, and the outcome was that he was banished from Rome.

erroneous doctrine and that they had come to Rome after they had been forced to flee Spain, Paris, and Venice, where they were wanted by the authorities for their false teaching and immoral living. Though Mudarra and friends never brought a formal charge against Ignatius, nevertheless, the slander they sowed had its effect, for the people now avoided them and were afraid to attend their sermons. Mudarra brought Miguel Landívar[11] into the picture by telling the governor, Benedetto Conversini,[12] that Miguel had known Ignatius in Paris and that he would reveal all secrets.

Ignatius appeared before Conversini carrying a letter that the same Miguel had written to him in Vicenza, dated September 12, 1537.[13] When the governor perused the letter, in which Miguel not only praised Ignatius but requested to join his group, Conversini immediately approached Miguel on the matter. Face to face with his own written testimony, Miguel admitted that he had been telling lies, and as a result the governor banished him from Rome.

Even though Ignatius had won the first skirmish, Mudarra was not willing to leave the field of battle, and thus he continued to spread his slanderous lies. As long as Ignatius was without a clear acquittal, the Romans continued to stay away from him and his companions. Since their

---

[11] Miguel Landívar was, at one time, Francis Xavier's servant in Paris. When Ignatius converted Xavier from his worldly ways, Miguel nurtured so great a hatred for Ignatius that he resolved to murder him, but failed in the attempt. He was in Venice in 1536 and went with the companions to Rome in 1537, but soon after left them. He once more appeared in Rome in 1538, this time as Ignatius' accuser, and was banished. See *FX* 188 n. 265.

[12] Conversini had been, since 1537, Bishop of Bertinoro. Before Paul III left Rome for Nice, March 1538, the pope appointed him governor and judge of Rome. See *FX* 423 n. 123.

[13] For this letter, see *Epistolae mixtae ex variis Europae locis ab anno 1537 ad 1556 scriptae* 1: *1537–1548* (*MHSI*) (Madrid: Aurial, 1898), 11–14.

Then Mudarra and Barreda began their persecution, alleging that the pilgrim and his companions were fugitives from Spain, from Paris, and from Venice. In the end, both of them confessed in the governor's presence and that of the

apostolate had been severely curtailed, Ignatius returned to Conversini and requested that his accusers be brought forward to prove their accusations publicly, and this the governor agreed to do. When Mudarra and friends were before the governor and papal legate, Cardinal Vincenzo Carafa,[14] they realized that they had now lost the battle and willingly acknowledged that they knew of nothing in Ignatius' teaching or way of life that was heretical or scandalous. With this admission, the governor and legate suggested that the case be dropped, but Ignatius insisted that a final sentence be rendered, for without such a sentence the specter of heresy would always overshadow them and their labors. In order that their work to help souls might bear fruit, an official exoneration was imperative, but Conversini did not see eye to eye with Ignatius, and so nothing was done about it.

Ignatius bided his time until Paul III returned to Rome in mid-August. The pope had been to Nice mediating a truce between Charles V and Francis I, and in the latter part of that month he went to his summer residence in Frascati. The determined Ignatius went to Frascati, secured an audience, and explained everything to His Holiness. Ignatius narrated the plans that he and his companions had in mind and related how he had been the victim of the Inquisition in Alcalá and Salamanca. He held nothing back. Finally, he asked that a complete investigation be made into their doctrine and life-style and that a sentence eventually be published. Under papal command, Conversini again took up the process, and after weeks of thorough investigation, during which nothing was found heretical in Ignatius' teaching or in his manner of life, the long-awaited sentence was finally published on November 18, 1538.[15]

With a favorable sentence to their credit, the companions, following the vow they had made in Montmartre (if unable to go to the Holy Land

---

[14] The cardinal became papal legate in Rome when Paul III set out for Nice.

[15] See *FD*, doc. 108.

legate, who was then in Rome, that they had nothing bad to say about them, or about their life-style, or about their teaching. The legate ordered silence to be imposed on the entire affair, but the pilgrim did not agree to this, but said that he wanted a definitive sentence issued. This was not to the legate's liking, or to that of the governor, or to those who were, from the beginning, well disposed toward the pilgrim. Finally, after several months, the pope returned to Rome. The

they would place themselves at the pope's disposal), went to visit Paul III sometime after the eighteenth and before the twenty-third of November. They offered themselves and their services to the pope for the good of the Church, saying that they were willing to go wherever the pope should decide to send them and to do whatever work the pope should decide to entrust to them. The pontiff accepted their humble offering, and within months he was to call on Ignatius and these same companions to supply missionaries to go to Siena, Parma, and India.

Since Ignatius' desire to celebrate his First Mass in the very land where Jesus had lived had never come to pass, he did the next best thing. At Santa Maria Maggiore in Rome, there was a Chapel of the Manger where a relic of Bethlehem was preserved, and there Ignatius and companions went on Christmas eve 1538. Surrounded by his closest friends and with eyes so filled with tears that he could hardly read the missal, Ignatius celebrated the Mass he had so long desired to celebrate.[16]

After Ignatius had narrated these events of 1538, he mentioned three particular works he had been instrumental in establishing in Rome. The first was an orphan society founded to distribute alms to the truly indigent—that is, to the sick, to beggars who were unable to work, and especially to orphans. The society was approved by Pope Paul III on February 7, 1541.[17] The second work of mercy that the early Jesuits sponsored was a residence for wives in moral danger and for fallen girls,

---

[16] See *GV* 459–60.

[17] By the bull *Altitudo*, Pope Paul III established the confraternity known as *Compagnia degli Orfani*. The first residence for orphans and abandoned children was next to the church of Santa Maria in Aquiro. The girls were later moved to a building adjacent to I Santi Quattro Coronati. See *GV* 528–29.

pilgrim went to speak with him at Frascati and set forth his several reasons, and the pope, now fully informed, ordered that sentence be given, and it was favorable to him, and so forth.

Through the pilgrim's help and that of his companions, several works of piety were initiated in Rome, for example,

where they were rehabilitated and prepared for positions in the world and for proper marriages. The papal bull establishing this residence was issued on February 16, 1543, and when the residence opened the following January, Ignatius named it after Saint Martha.[18] Though the everyday operation of the residence was in the hands of a confraternity founded especially for this purpose, Ignatius had charge of the spiritual government of the house. The final work of piety that Ignatius mentioned was the establishment of a house for catechumens. Many Jews and Muslims in Rome, who desired to become Catholics, found that as long as they nurtured this desire they were unable to remain at home; hence they lived together in a residence where the Jesuits served as catechists. This apostolate received the pope's approbation on February 19, 1543.[19]

Realizing that Gonçalves da Câmara would shortly be leaving Rome and being unable to complete his narration, Ignatius told him that Master Nadal would fill him in on all that remained, for Nadal was going to Spain and Gonçalves da Câmara was to be his traveling companion.

---

[18] By the bull *Divina summaque Dei bonitas*, the pope established the *Compagnia della Grazia* (*GV* 531–33). See Charles Chauvin, "La Maison Sainte Marthe: Ignace et les prostituées de Rome", *Christus* 38 (1991): 117–26. Then in 1545 Pope Paul III orally approved the *Compagnia delle vergini miserabili* (Confraternity of Unfortunate Single Women), to keep these endangered girls from following in their mothers' footsteps. It was founded by Ignatius in a house next to the church of Santa Caterina dei Funari. The confraternity was officially erected by Pope Pius IV on January 6, 1560. See *GV* 333.

[19] By the bull *Illius qui pro dominici*, Pope Paul III canonically established houses for Jewish catechumens, one for men and another for women. Prior to this Ignatius had been taking care of Jewish and Muslim catechumens in the Jesuit residence and then in a house provided for them by Margaret of Austria. This bull now gave formal approbation to Ignatius' apostolate among catechumens and provided for two houses, one for men and another for women. See *GV* 538.

the house for catechumens, that of Saint Martha, the orphan society, and so on. As for the rest, Master Nadal can tell you about that.

99. After he had narrated these matters, I asked the pilgrim on October 20, about the Exercises and the Constitutions, because I wanted to know how he had written them. He told me that he had not composed the Exercises all at one time, but perceiving certain things happening in his soul, and finding them helpful, he thought that they might also be helpful to others, and so he set them down in writing, for example, the examination of conscience with its series of lines, and so on. He told me that he had especially derived the elections from that diversity of spirits and thoughts he had experienced when he was at Loyola, still suffering with his bad leg. As for the Constitutions, he told me that he would speak to me about them that evening.

That same day, before supper, he called for me and seemed to be more recollected than usual. He made a solemn avowal,

99–101. Now that Ignatius had finished his story, Gonçalves da Câmara hurriedly asked him about the composition of the Spiritual Exercises and the Constitutions. As for the former, Ignatius said that they were written over a period of time and were based on his own experiences in prayer. Whatever he found helpful he recorded so that these exercises might prove helpful to others. The Constitutions were likewise written under the influence of prayer, for when Ignatius celebrated Mass he would present the point under consideration to God and request enlightenment, and if he were coming to a decision, he asked for confirmation. During the years he was occupied writing the Constitutions and perfecting them, Ignatius was the recipient of countless mystical graces, all of which he recorded in his *Spiritual Journal*,[20] of which only a fragment remains today, covering the time between February 2, 1544, and February 27, 1545. This fragment

[20] *Spiritual Journal of Ignatius Loyola, February 2, 1544, to February 27, 1545*, trans. William J. Young, S.J. (Woodstock Md.: Woodstock College, 1958).

the gist of which was to inform me that his intention had
been to be sincere in all that he had related; that he was
certain that he did not exaggerate in anything; that he had
often offended God after he had begun to serve Him but
had never consented to mortal sin; and that his devotion,
that is, his ease in finding God, was always increasing, now
more than ever in his entire life. At whatever time or hour
he wanted to find God, he found Him. Also that he now has
many visions, especially those, as have been mentioned above,
of seeing Christ as the sun. This often occurred when he
was speaking of important matters, and those visions came
to him as corroborations.

100. When he celebrated Mass he also had many visions,
and when he was writing the Constitutions he had them
quite frequently. This he can prove very easily because every
day he noted what was taking place in his soul and all this is
found written down. He then showed me a rather large packet
of writings, and from these he read to me a sizable amount.
For the most part they were visions that he had had con-
firming certain points in the Constitutions. Sometimes he
saw God the Father, at other times all three Persons of the
Trinity, and at other times our Lady, who was at times in-
terceding for him and at times strengthening him.

He especially spoke to me about certain items under deliberation and for which he had celebrated Mass every day
for forty days and daily had shed many tears. The question

appears to be much less than that "large packet of writings" from which
Ignatius read excerpts to Gonçalves da Câmara. It is unknown how
the greater part of the journal became lost, or whether Ignatius himself
had destroyed it. Certainly, when Gonçalves da Câmara asked to take
them to his room to read at his leisure, Ignatius would not part with
them. He probably felt that he had already revealed more than he had
intended.

was whether a church should have any income, and if the Society could make use of that income.

101. The method he followed when writing the Constitutions was to celebrate Mass every day and present the point under consideration to God and to pray over it. He always had tears when he prayed or celebrated Mass.

I wanted to see all these papers on the Constitutions and asked him to let me have them for a while, but he would not.

APPENDIX I

PREFACE OF FATHER NADAL[1]

1. I, and many other fathers, have heard our Father Ignatius say that he had asked God to grant him three graces before departing this life. First, that the Apostolic See confirm the Institute of the Society; second, the same for the Spiritual Exercises; third, that he be able to write the Constitutions.

2. Remembering this, and seeing that he had received all three graces,[2] I began to fear that he would be called from us to go to a better life. Since I knew that the holy father-founders of monastic communities had been accustomed to leave their sons some admonition, as a testament, to help them grow in virtue, I waited for the opportune moment to ask the same of Father Ignatius.

One day in 1551,[3] when we were together, Father Ignatius said to me: "Just now I was higher than heaven." I

---

[1] This is a translation of the Latin text in *FN* 1:354–63; it appears at the bottom of those pages. A Spanish translation of the same is in *OC* 85–86. The substance of the following notes is based on those that accompany the Spanish translation.

[2] On September 27, 1540, the Society of Jesus received the official confirmation of Pope Paul III with the bull *Regimini militantis Ecclesiae*. The book of the *Spiritual Exercises* was approved by the same pontiff in his letter *Pastoralis officii cura* of July 31, 1548. And Ignatius had completed writing the Society's Constitutions in March 1552.

[3] *OC* 87 n. 3 suggests that the date should be 1552, since Nadal spent all of 1551 in Sicily and only returned to Rome on January 5, 1552.

understood this to mean that he had experienced some ecstasy or rapture, as it frequently happened to him. With the deepest respect I asked him: "Father, what do you mean?" But he changed the conversation to something else. Thinking that this was the suitable moment, I begged the Father to be kind enough to tell us how the Lord had guided him from the beginning of his conversion, so that his explanation could serve us as a testament and paternal instruction. Thus, I said to him: "Since God has granted you the three graces you desired before your death, we fear, Father, that you will soon be called to heaven."

3. The Father offered business matters as his excuse, saying that he had neither the inclination nor the time for it. He added, however: "Offer three Masses for this intention, you, Polanco,[4] and Ponce,[5] and after you have prayed tell me what you think." I answered: "Father, we will be of the same opinion as we now are." But he replied with great gentleness: "Do what I tell you!" We celebrated the three Masses and reported to him that we were of the same mind, and he then promised to do what we had asked.

The following year,[6] after I had again returned from Sicily, and, being about to be sent to Spain, I asked the Father if he had done anything. "Nothing", he said. When I returned from Spain in 1554, I asked him once more. He had

---

[4] At this time Polanco was Ignatius' secretary.

[5] Ponce de Cogordan was a Frenchman who entered the Society as a priest in 1541, made his solemn profession in Rome in 1553, was treasurer of the Jesuit community in Rome, and was back in Paris by 1560. He died there in 1582.

[6] According to OC 88 n. 5, this should be 1553. After making his profession in Rome on March 25, 1552, Nadal was again sent to Sicily. In January 1553 he was once more in Rome, and then in April of that year he set out for Spain and Portugal to promulgate the Society's Constitutions among the Jesuits in those countries.

not yet begun.[7] I do not know what impelled me, but I insisted with the Father: "It is now going on four years that not only have I asked you, but also other fathers, for you to explain to us, Father, how the Lord formed you from the beginning of your conversion, for we are confident that knowing this would be most beneficial to us and to the Society. But since I see that you will not grant it to us, I dare to make this statement: If you grant the request we so earnestly desire, we will put it to our best use, and if you do not grant it, our spirits will not be thereby dejected, but we will have the same confidence in the Lord as if you had written everything down."

4. The Father did not answer anything, but—I think it was the same day—he called Father Luis Gonçalves da Câmara to him and began his narration. This father, endowed with an excellent memory, afterward wrote it down. This Father Luis was an elector at the General Congregation,[8] and at the same he was elected assistant to Father General Laínez. Later he became tutor in literature and Christian morals to Sebastian, King of Portugal. He is a father known for his piety and outstanding virtue. Father Gonçalves wrote a part in Spanish and a part in Italian, depending on the scribes he had at his disposal. Father Annibal de Coudret,[9] a learned and pious man, made the Latin translation. Both the author and the translator are still alive.

---

[7] Nadal wrote this Preface between 1561 and 1567. He had evidently forgotten that Ignatius had begun to narrate his life to Gonçalves da Câmara in August-September 1553.

[8] The first General Congregation, which elected Father Diego Laínez general of the Society, took place in 1558.

[9] Annibal de Coudret, a Frenchman, was born in 1525, entered the Society in 1546, was sent to Sicily in 1548, and returned to Rome in 1558. While stationed at the Roman College he translated Gonçalves da Câmara's Spanish-Italian text into Latin. In 1561 he returned to France and died at Avignon in 1599.

APPENDIX II

CHRONOLOGY OF EVENTS IN THE
LIFE OF IGNATIUS OF LOYOLA

1491	– born at Loyola Castle, prior to October 23
1505	
October 23	– acts as witness in the sale of a horse in Azpeitia
1506 (?)	– in service to Juan Velázquez de Cuéllar of Arévalo, treasurer to King Ferdinand
1515	
February 20	– youthful escapade in Azpeitia, with charges subsequently brought against him and his brother
1516	
January 23	– death of King Ferdinand
March 14	– Charles becomes king
1517	
August 12	– Juan Velázquez de Cuéllar dies
End of year	– in service to Antonio Manrique de Lara, Duke of Nájera, Viceroy of Navarre
1520	
September	– participates in quelling minor revolt in Nájera
1521	
January–April	– helps to bring peace to provincial factions in Guipúzcoa
May 17–18	– hastens to Pamplona to defend the city against French
19	– convinces commander to defend fortress
23–24	– right leg is wounded during siege
	– fortress at Pamplona surrenders to French

June 2–5	– leaves Pamplona for Loyola Castle
17–20	– arrives at Loyola Castle
24	– receives the last sacraments
28 midnight	– health begins to improve
August–September	– begins reading a life of Christ and those of the saints; undergoes conversion and has vision of our Lady

1522

End of February	– leaves Loyola on way to Montserrat
March 21	– arrives at Montserrat
22–24	– prepares for general confession
24	– sets aside his fine clothing for pilgrim's tunic; at midnight begins vigil before our Lady's altar
25	– early morning leaves Montserrat and arrives in Manresa, where he lives life of prayer and penance
August–September (?)	– extraordinary illumination on the shores of the Cardoner; undergoes interior transformation

1523

Mid-February	– departs Manresa
17–18	– arrives in Barcelona on way to Holy Land
Mid-March	– departs for Italy
20–22	– arrives in Gaeta, Italy
29	– arrives in Rome on Palm Sunday
April 13–14	– departs Rome for Venice
May 14(?)	– arrives in Venice
July 14	– departs for Cyprus on the *Negrona*
August 19	– departs Las Salinas, Cyprus
25	– arrives at Jaffa
September 4	– enters Jerusalem; visits the Holy Places
23	– departs Jerusalem for Jaffa
October 3	– sails from Jaffa
14–28	– on island of Cyprus
Early November	– sails for Venice

1524

Mid-January	– arrives in Venice
Early February	– departs for Genoa and Barcelona

Late February– early March	– arrives in Barcelona; visits Manresa; begins studies
1525	– spends year in studies in Barcelona
1526 July (?) November 19	– goes to Alcalá for studies – first process initiated against Ignatius
1527 March 6 April 18/19 May 2–21 June 1 21 Early July Mid-July End of July August 20–22 Mid-September	– second process in Alcalá – put into prison – third process – released from prison – departs Alcalá for Valladolid – visits Archbishop Fonseca in Valladolid; goes to Salamanca – arrives in Salamanca – meets with Dominican friars at San Esteban, then imprisonment – released from prison – leaves Salamanca for Barcelona, then to Paris
1528 February 2	– arrives in Paris: begins studies at Collège de Montaigu
1529 Lent September October 1	– first begging tour in Flanders – visits Rouen – moves to Collège de Sainte-Barbe; meets Favre and Xavier; begins study of philosophy
1530 August–September	– second begging tour in Flanders
1531 August–September	– third begging tour in Flanders; visits London
1532 January	– receives bachelor of arts degree
1533 March 13 October	– passes examination for licentiate degree – begins study of theology with Dominicans

1534
January   – gives Exercises to Favre
Spring   – gives Exercises to Laínez and Salmerón; later to
                        Rodrigues and Bobadilla
August 15   – vows at Montmartre
September   – gives Exercises to Xavier

1535
March 14   – receives diploma of master of arts
Late March   – defends himself against accusation of heresy be-
                        fore Valentín Liévin
Early April   – leaves Paris for Spain
April 23   – arrives in Azpeitia
Late July   – departs Azpeitia
August–September   – visits Obanos, Almazán, Sigüenza, Madrid,
                        Toledo, Valencia
October–November   – visits Charterhouse of Val de Cristo; leaves
                        Valencia for Genoa
Mid-November   – arrives Genoa; starts journey to Bologna
December 11–18(?)   – ill in Bologna
End of December   – leaves Bologna; arrives Venice

1536   – spends year in Venice studying theology and giv-
                        ing Exercises

1537
January 8   – companions arrive from Paris and work in
                        hospitals
March 10   – companions leave for Rome; Ignatius remains in
                        Venice
        25   – companions arrive in Rome
April 3   – audience with Pope Paul III
Early May   – depart Rome for Venice
Mid-May   – arrival in Venice
June 24   – Ignatius and five companions are ordained to
                        priesthood
July 25   – Ignatius, Favre, and Laínez leave for Vicenza;
                        others leave for other cities
End of August   – travels with Favre to Bassano to visit Rodrigues,
                        who is ill

September–October	- companions celebrate their first Masses in Vicenza; decide on their ministries and the name of their group
October 13	- declaration of Ignatius' innocence given in Venice
End of October	- leaves with Favre and Laínez for Rome
Mid-November	- vision at La Storta; arrives in Rome and lives near Trinità dei Monti

1538

March–April	- At Monte Cassino giving Exercises to Pedro Ortiz
End of April	- companions arrive in Rome; group moves to residence near Ponte Sisto
May	- persecution begins
End of August	- goes to Frascati to visit Pope Paul III and requests definitive sentence
November 18	- sentence exonerating Ignatius and companions published
November 18–23	- the young Society offers its services to Pope Paul III in accord with vow at Montmartre
December 25	- Ignatius celebrates his first Mass in Chapel of the Manger in Santa Maria Maggiore

1539

Mid-March–June 24	- deliberations on whether to form a new religious congregation
End of June–early July	- Ignatius prepares "Formula of the Institute"
September 3	- Pope Paul III grants oral approval for "Formula"

1540

March 4	- Simão Rodrigues leaves Rome for Portugal
March 16	- Francis Xavier leaves Rome for Portugal and India
September 27	- confirmation of the Society by papal bull *Regimini militantis Ecclesiae*

1541

| February 7 | - papal bull confirming the confraternity for orphans |

March 4	–	first companions discuss the writing of Constitutions for the new Society
10	–	Ignatius and Codure given task of writing Constitutions
April 8	–	Ignatius is elected general, but declines
13	–	is again elected, but requests time for prayer
19	–	accepts election as general
22	–	Ignatius and companions make their solemn profession in Chapel of Our Lady in St. Paul Outside-the-Walls

1542
March 21	–	papal brief in favor of converted Jews

1543
February 16	–	papal bull establishing House of Saint Martha
19	–	papal bull establishing house for catechumens in Rome

1544
January	–	House of Saint Martha opens
March 14	–	papal bull, *Iniunctum nobis*, again confirms the Society and no longer limits membership to sixty

1545
June 3	–	papal brief granting faculties and privileges to the Society

1546
June 5	–	papal brief permitting Society to accept spiritual and temporal coadjutors
August 1	–	death of Pierre Favre in Rome
October 1	–	apostolic constitution forbidding female branch of the Society
25	–	Portugal is made first province in the Society; Simão Rodrigues named provincial

1547
May 7	–	Ignatius writes letter on perfection
September 1	–	Antonio Araoz is named first provincial of Spain

1548
July 31	–	Pope Paul III praises and approves the Spiritual Exercises
September 11	–	first printing of the *Spiritual Exercises* in Rome

1549

February 1	- first missionaries go to Brazil
16	- preparations made for Peter Canisius, Claude Jay, and Alfonso Salmerón to go to Germany
June 27	- Ignatius contemplates founding Roman College and building a new church for the Society
October 10	- India becomes a province with Francis Xavier as provincial

1550

July 21	- Pope Julius III's bull *Exposcit debitum*, confirming the Society

1551

January	- professed fathers gather in Rome to discuss Constitutions
30	- because of ill health Ignatius submits his resignation, but not accepted
February 22	- Roman College inaugurated
August 1	- Ignatius contemplates establishing a German College in Rome
December 5	- Italy becomes a province with Paschase Broët as provincial
End of December	- Diego Miro is appointed provincial of Portugal

1552

January 1	- Simão Rodrigues is appointed provincial of Aragon
February 1	- Jerónimo Doménech made first provincial of Sicily
March	- Ignatius finishes writing Constitutions
March 25	- Jerónimo Nadal appointed to promulgate Constitutions in Sicily
August 31	- papal bull establishing German College in Rome

1553

March 26	- famous letter on obedience to the Jesuits in Coimbra
April 10	- Nadal appointed to promulgate Constitutions in Spain and Portugal
July 9	- Ignatius establishes Brazil with Emmanuel de Nóbrega provincial

| End of August | – Ignatius begins to dictate his "autobiography" to Gonçalves da Cámara |

1554

January 7	– Spain divided into three provinces: Aragón, Castile, and Bética
June 14	– entrusts the construction of the Society's new church to Michelangelo Buonarotti
October 6	– work begins on the church but continues only until 1555
November 1	– Ignatius asks priests in Rome to choose a vicar general to assist him in governing Society; he confirms the election of Jerónimo Nadal

1555

| August | – France becomes a province |

1556

June 7	– Peter Canisius appointed first provincial of Germany
July 31	– Ignatius dies at 5:30 A.M.
August 1	– buried in church of Our Lady della Strada

1609

| July 27 | – beatified by Pope Paul V |

1622

| March 12 | – canonized by Pope Gregory XV |

APPENDIX III

SELECT BIBLIOGRAPHY

On Ignatius of Loyola

Brodrick, James. *Saint Ignatius Loyola: The Pilgrim Years 1491–1538*. Reprint. San Francisco: Ignatius Press, 1998.

Caraman, Philip. *Ignatius Loyola: A Biography of the Founder of the Jesuits*. San Francisco: Harper and Row, 1990.

Dalmases, Candido de. *Ignatius of Loyola, Founder of the Jesuits: His Life and Work*. St. Louis: Institute of Jesuit Sources, 1985.

Dudon, Paul. *St. Ignatius of Loyola*. Translated by William J. Young. Milwaukee: Bruce, 1949.

Purcell, Mary. *The First Jesuit: St. Ignatius Loyola (1491–1556)*. Chicago: Loyola University, 1981.

Rahner, Karl, and Paul Imhof. *Ignatius of Loyola*. New York: Collins, 1979.

Ravier, André. *Ignatius of Loyola and the Founding of the Society of Jesus*. San Francisco: Ignatius Press, 1987.

Tellechea Idígoras, José Ignacio. *Ignatius of Loyola: The Pilgrim Saint*. Translated and edited by Cornelius Michael Buckley. Chicago: Loyola University, 1994.

On Ignatian Spirituality

Brou, Alexandre. *The Ignatian Way to God*. Translated by William J. Young. Milwaukee: Bruce, 1952.

Finding God in All Things: Essays in Ignatian Spirituality selected from Christus. Translated by William J. Young. Chicago: Regnery, 1958.

Gill, Henry Vincent. *Jesuit Spirituality: Leading Ideas of the Spiritual Exercises*. Dublin: H. M. Gill, 1935.

Guibert, Joseph de. *The Jesuits: Their Spiritual Doctrine and Practice; A Historical Study*. Translated by William J. Young. Edited by George E. Ganss. Chicago: Institute of Jesuit Sources, 1964.

Maruca, Dominic. *Instruments in the Hand of God: A Study in the Spirituality of St. Ignatius*. Rome: Gregorian University, 1963.

Peeters, Louis. *An Ignatian Approach to Divine Union*. Translated by Hillard L. Brozowski. Milwaukee: Bruce, 1956.

Puhl, L. *The Spiritual Exercises of St. Ignatius: A New Translation*. Westminster, Md.: Newman, 1951.

Rahner, Hugo. *St. Ignatius the Theologian*. Translated by Michael Barry. New York: Herder and Herder, 1968.

———. *The Spirituality of St. Ignatius of Loyola: An Account of Its Historical Development*. Translated by Francis John Smith. Chicago: Loyola University, 1980.

ABBREVIATIONS

FD   =   *Fontes Documentales de S. Ignatio de Loyola: Documenta de S. Ignatii familia et patria, iuventute, primis sociis (MHSI* 115). Edited by Candidus de Dalmases, S. I. [S. J.] Rome: Institutum Historicum Societatis Iesu, 1977.

FN   =   *Fontes Narrativi de S. Ignatio de Loyola et de Societatis Iesu initiis.* Vol. 1, *Narrationes scriptae ante annum 1557 (MHSI* 66). Edited by Dionysius Fernandez Zapico, S. I. [S. J.], and Candidus de Dalmases, S. I. [S. J.] Rome: Monumenta Historica Soc. Iesu, 1943; Vol. 2, *Narrationes scriptae annis 1557-1574 (MHSI* 73). Edited by Candidus de Dalmases, S. I. [S. J.]. Rome: Monumenta Historica Soc. Iesu, 1951. Vol. 4, *Vita Ignatii Loyolae auctore Petro de Ribadeneyra (MHSI* 93). Edited by Candidus de Dalmases, S. I. [S. J.] Rome: Monumenta Historica Soc. Iesu, 1965.

FX   =   Schurhammer, Georg, S. J. *Francis Xavier, His Life, His Times.* Vol. 1, *Europe 1506–1541.* Translated by M. Joseph Costelloe, S. J. Rome: Jesuit Historical Institute, 1973.

GP   =   Gilbert, M. "Le Pèlerinage d'Iñigo à Jérusalem en 1523". *Nouvelle Revue Théologique* 112 (1990): 660–85.

GV   =   García-Villoslada, Ricardo, S. J. *San Ignazio de Loyola: Nueva Biografía.* Madrid: Biblioteca de Autores Cristianos, 1986.

IdL   =   Leturia, Pedro, S. J. *Iñigo de Loyola.* Translated by Aloysius J. Owen, S. J. Syracuse: Le Moyne College, 1949.

IL   =   Dudon, Paul, S. J. *St. Ignatius of Loyola.* Translated by William J. Young, S. J. Chicago: Bruce, 1949.

LIL   =   *Letters of St. Ignatius of Loyola.* Translated by William J. Young, S. J. Chicago: Loyola University, 1959.

LW   =   Rahner, Hugo, S. J. *St. Ignatius of Loyola: Letters to Women.* Translated by Kathleen Pond and S. A. H. Weetman. New York: Herder and Herder, 1960.

MHSI   =   *Monumenta Historica Societatis Iesu.* Madrid-Rome: 1894–.

MR = Matt, Leonard von, and Hugo Rahner. *St. Ignatius of Loyola: A Pictorial Biography*. Chicago: Henry Regnery, 1956.

OC = *San Ignacio de Loyola: Obras Completas*. 4th revised edition. Edited by Ignacio Iparraguirre, S. I. [S. J.], and Candido de Dalmases, S. I. [S. J.]. Madrid: Biblioteca de Autores Cristianos, 1982.

PY = Brodrick, James, S. J. *Saint Ignatius Loyola: The Pilgrim Years 1491–1538*. 1956. Reprint, San Francisco: Ignatius Press, 1998.